THE BATTLE WORTH
Fighting

Raising Faith Guided Children
In A Single Parent Home

JULIE ANN ALLEN

WESTBOW
PRESS®
A DIVISION OF THOMAS NELSON
& ZONDERVAN

WestBow Press books may be ordered through booksellers or by contacting:

WestBow Press
A Division of Thomas Nelson & Zondervan
1663 Liberty Drive
Bloomington, IN 47403
www.westbowpress.com
1 (866) 928-1240

Because of the dynamic nature of the Internet, any web addresses or links contained in this book may have changed since publication and may no longer be valid. The views expressed in this work are solely those of the author and do not necessarily reflect the views of the publisher, and the publisher hereby disclaims any responsibility for them.

Any people depicted in stock imagery provided by Getty Images are models, and such images are being used for illustrative purposes only. Certain stock imagery © Getty Images.

ISBN: 978-1-9736-4266-4 (sc)
ISBN: 978-1-9736-4267-1 (hc)
ISBN: 978-1-9736-4265-7 (e)

Library of Congress Control Number: 2018912119

Print information available on the last page.

WestBow Press rev. date: 10/10/2018

This book is dedicated to
CarleeAnn and Chase

The two amazing people who gave me the
best job I will ever do, and the greatest joy on this planet;
because they call me "Mom."

CONTENTS

FOREWORD

When people think about their life and future very few dream of being a single parent. Most hope to find their soul mate, move to the suburbs and raise the perfect family. The harsh reality is that more and more people are raising children alone due to loss, divorce or by choice. But how does someone navigate the terrible twos and the tumultuous teenage years and everything in between by themselves? It's hard enough to raise children to become happy, healthy adults with two parents, how can someone do it successfully alone?

As the child of a single parent I have seen first-hand the struggle that my mom faced trying to raise my brother and me. Staying up into the wee hours of the morning helping us study, entertaining our phases or obsessions, and sharing in our joy over exciting milestones and our pain when failures seemed too disappointing to handle.

And she had to do it alone.

There was no one there to be a soundboard when tough decisions needed to be made, nobody could empty the dishwasher while she helped one of us prep for a spelling test, she had to raise two kids without a teammate, partner, or even an adult conversation to save her from the endless conversations about dinosaurs or the prom.

At the time I couldn't comprehend all of the sacrifices my mom made so that my brother and I could have a happy, healthy childhood. I don't know how many girl's nights she had to turn down because she couldn't get a babysitter, the shoes she would've loved to treat herself with but didn't because she needed to save money for camp fees, or how many moments she felt completely, utterly alone.

It was only when I grew up, went away to college, got married and moved away that I started to realized just how hard the past 16 years must have been for my mom and the countless other single parents trying to raise grounded, godly children.

The modern world we live in has changed and in turn has changed how families interact with one another. Long gone are the days when families engaged in conversation at a restaurant, discussing what happened at school, or working together on the word search in the kids menu. More often than not each person at a table will have their own electronic device to keep them quiet and entertained.

It's hard to convince people that it's not all about the "likes" and that the false sense of reality we get from social media is a façade that people project to make their lives seem perfect. How do you teach children to become people who spread God's love and care for others, rather than focusing on themselves?

I know I am lucky. My mom created a happy, faith-based and balanced environment for us to grow up in. We had open, honest conversations about the challenges, temptations and struggles that we faced in our everyday lives. Yes we had our fair share of arguments and disagreements, but we learned the importance of forgiveness, patience and love. She instilled in us self-confidence, respect and a faith in God that has carried us through the pitfalls we all face in life.

The Battle Worth Fighting is her story and our story as a family. It is an honest look at the struggle that it is to raise children to become not only happy, healthy adults but people grounded in God's will.

CarleeAnn Allen Hatton

October 1, 2018

PREFACE

A father to the fatherless, a defender of widows, is God in his holy Dwelling.

—Psalm 68:5 (NIV)

One day recently, when I was feeling lonely and beat by the demands of life and my very long solo flight, I was honest with my teenage son. I told him I was feeling defeated. He offered some amazingly comforting and wise counsel, pointing out things I should be proud of, and then he said, "You are one of the best parents I know—probably one of the best parents in the entire world! It's like you should be in a book or something." He was stating what I have felt God speaking to my heart for a very long time, telling me to put into words how God has guided and protected me as I have tried the best way I knew how to raise the children I am blessed to call my kids. Despite my son's heartfelt accolade, I know I am not one of the best parents in the entire world. But I did get to hear my teenage son say he thought I might be. More than that, he didn't even ask for anything. It doesn't get much better than that!

When I faced raising two children as a single widowed mom, I was filled with fear. I was keenly aware of all my limitations and inabilities, and the future seemed daunting. I truly felt that there was no possible way I could manage. I read a few books on parenting and family by Christian authors, and they all had the same theme: the role of the father in my children's lives was vital. According to these books, without a father in their lives, my children only had a 33 percent chance of success. I will forever be grateful to John and Staci Eldridge and the books *Wild at Heart* and *Captivating* for the wisdom and hope provided within those works. Throughout my account of raising Christian children in a single-parent home, there will be attitudes and thoughts that, while not direct quotations, clearly are rooted in *Wild at Heart* and *Captivating*, as those books have shaped so much of my parenting. After reading these two books, I immediately began shaping all I spoke of with my children and my own attitudes with the conviction that God is the Father who will not let us down. God is the Father who loves us unconditionally and has good things in store for us. God is the Father who will always be there with each of us. I have raised two children as a single widowed mom with God as my children's Father.

> Sing to God, sing in praise of his name, extol him who rides on the clouds; rejoice before him—his name is the lord. A father to the fatherless, a defender of widows, is God in his holy dwelling. (Psalm 68:4–5 NIV)

I remember sitting at my late husband's funeral and praying fervently, "God, I give you these children just like Abraham gave you Isaac. I can't raise them alone, so you will have to take them." This book is an account of God's answer to my prayer and all I have learned as I traveled this road.

Please know that I am just like any other parent. I don't claim to have all the answers, and I have made more than my fair share of mistakes. I recognize that there is not one perfect solution to every challenge we face as parents. The challenges come in a wide variety of categories, discipline, finances, schedules, and school study habits—and the list goes on. The solutions and ways parents address these challenges come in an equally wide range of options. But one thing I know—God is the Father to the fatherless. I hope we can all recognize the heart of the message in that scripture. It has come to mean to me that God is the loving authority in my children's lives and in my life. God's will and God's direction is what should be followed. Additionally God's provisions and protections are what we praise and give thanks for every day. God can provide all we need in every situation and will care for us beyond our expectations if we allow him to do so.

I have spent the past fifteen years raising two children with only one earthly parent in their lives. The most important aspect of my approach has been to firmly and consistently teach them that they can count on God as their Father and that he will never fail them or forsake them. Most importantly, I have tried to teach them that when they look to God for approval, they will always find love and grace and the approval we all so desperately seek. God is the ultimate authority telling my daughter she is lovely, the ultimate authority telling my son he has what it takes to be a man! God has provided honorable and godly men and women in the lives of our family who have continually demonstrated to my children what it is to be a person of faith. God provided situations for our family that would prove to my children that he created them lovely and capable. Not all these situations in our lives were joyful and easy. As a family we faced many challenging and difficult situations. Not all of them were moments we would have chosen for ourselves. But all of them were covered with God's fingerprints.

God does not give us overwhelming circumstances; God gives us the strength as we live to overcome those circumstances and live well beyond them. The condition of living in a fallen world generates so many circumstances that can feel overwhelming. I am certain that God did not want me to be in a position to raise two children alone. I wrote the book *You Only Think God Is Silent* to speak to that topic. This struggle to raise God-directed and faith-guided children in a single-parent home was not something God would have chosen for me or for any one of us. God has provided all I needed so I would know that I am not alone. God wants for each one of us to know we are not alone. Yes, at night when I lay my head down to sleep, I am physically alone in the room, but I am never on this journey alone. I have had the comfort, guidance, and provisions of a loving God, and the empowerment of a mighty God, to enable me to live well beyond this overwhelming circumstance. And more than that, I have the overwhelming joy of raising two amazing and incredible children who have God's fingerprints all over them!

In scripture we find many miracles performed by Jesus. As we read, we see Jesus often required action from the recipient of those miracles. Jesus commanded an action, and then the overcoming of the overwhelming occurred. Some were instructed to fill the clay jars with water, and then there was wine at the wedding feast. The blind man had to wash the mud from his eyes, and then he could see. This is the same for us. When the call seems too daunting or too overwhelming, step forth in faith, and the miraculous overcoming will begin! We all have children around us who have God's fingerprints all over them. And the exciting news is that grace gives each of us access to the same mighty power of God to overcome this overwhelming circumstance we call parenting.

ALONE IN THE STANDS

The Lord himself goes before you and will be with you;
he will never leave you nor forsake you. Do not be afraid;
do not be discouraged.

—Deuteronomy 31:8 (NIV)

The stadium was full of moms with bling-covered jerseys on, and each had a big pinned-on button with her son's picture on it. The stadium also had dads in work attire straight from the office. It was all new to me. Seventh-grade football in Texas—this was the first home game. This was my own son's first attempt at football. I was more accustomed to the Saturday soccer-mom scene, and this felt like foreign territory. Honestly, I could not understand the hype. I sat down to watch the game, feeling awkward and very alone. The game started, and very quickly our team scored. My son put his helmet on and stepped on the field. I suddenly felt nervous for him. He was the kicker. In seventh grade, the point after the touchdown kick is worth two points, not just one. This meant every kick counted a little more. I was almost a nervous wreck by the time they set up for the kick. He kicked, and the ball sailed through the uprights. The crowd cheered, the cheerleaders hit play on the sound system, and the school fight song started to play as the cheerleaders launched into their dance routine. Without realizing why, my eyes filled with tears. I instantly realized why the moms had the big picture buttons, and yes, I wanted one! I realized why the dads had come straight from the office, and I wanted my son's dad there. I didn't have a big button, but I could fix that. His dad wasn't there—and never would be there to see him kick a point after or a field goal, or to see any of his or his sister's many accomplishments. I sat there crying tears of joy, pride, and grief—just like I had at so many events for each of my children before. And I knew it wouldn't be the last time either.

When my children were small (my daughter, seven, and my son, a five-month-old infant), I was widowed. I honestly don't know where the years have gone. Now my daughter is an adult and my son is a teenager, and I am still a single parent doing the best I can to raise Christian children in a single-parent home. We are a family with God as Dad and head of household. Many statistics are available about the daunting odds my children face. Reason, logic, and psychological studies say that my children are more likely to struggle and fail. My faith counters that. My faith tells me that these are God's children. My faith and my experience tell me that God is greater than the statistics.

I am not going to pretend my children are perfect. I am certain that if I allowed them to contribute a chapter to this work titled "Mistakes My Mother Made," it would be a long chapter. I am also certain that by prayer and with consistent intention to follow God's leading, grace, and love, I now see two Christian people whom I am blessed to call my children. I often look at who they are becoming and marvel at all that God has done, all that God is doing, and all that I am confident God will do in our lives. God is doing a mighty work in our lives.

I will never forget the day my daughter came home from science club with a box that contained the parts for building a small wood car. When I opened the box, there was a block of wood. A perfectly square wood block, some metal rods, and four plastic wheels were all of the contents of the box. Somehow, I was supposed to help her transform this into a racecar. I looked at this "kit" and asked God, "Really! You want me to build a car?" I was overwhelmed and completely out of my league. I couldn't even make dinner with great success, so how was I going to build a car?! The next Sunday while in Sunday school class, I was sharing my complete lack of knowledge and skill in the area of building wooden cars and discussed how thoroughly overwhelmed I was by the task. One of the class members volunteered to partner with my daughter and build her car. And that is how God works. I have lived that a thousand times over as these past years have flown by. When I felt overwhelmed by a task in front of me, God would provide exactly the help needed. Although raising a seven-year-old and an infant to college age and young

2

adulthood seemed like an impossibly long journey, God has made it an amazing journey. And the time has passed so quickly. Almost every time I walk past my daughter's bedroom, I gaze in and long for that young girl who would read every book she could find and talk to me about each moment of her day. I am awestruck by the woman she has become, and I deeply treasure every moment of her years with me. I even treasure the moments filled with crying and arguing. The years flew by so fast that I can only say, like so many others do, that I blinked and she grew up.

Our journey and my life as a single mom is undoubtedly much like the lives of many single parents. I have identified areas where God had led me to be purposeful and intentional in parenting efforts. When I sit among the moms in the stadium, I know that my son is only going to be living in my home for a short time longer. I will soon have two rooms to gaze into and remember. I want to treasure every moment and watch every game—and even get a big button pin with his picture on it! When I was widowed, the task of raising these two young children as a single mom seemed absolutely overwhelming. Yet in what seems like the blink of an eye, I was watching my daughter stride into her high school graduation wearing a mass of honor cords and a proud smile. Too soon she had moved into a college dorm, and then she was walking across that university graduation stage. I know it won't be very long before the placekicker on that middle school football field does the same.

I can remember walking into my late husband's funeral, holding my daughter's hand and carrying my son in his infant car seat; I was thinking that I could not possibly get them through high school alone. What I have learned so well is that I didn't; I have not been alone. God has provided for me, consoled, led, and comforted me, and performed untold numbers of miracles. God is the reason for my daughter's proud smile, academic success, and scholarship to college. God is the authority in our household.

A couple of years after that first point after touchdown kick, I was sitting at a party watching the Super Bowl. It was so fun to be with other adults watching the game. It was the first time in many years that I had watched the Super Bowl this way. It happened because my son had been invited to this party, and the parents of the kids invited were also included. I was enjoying myself so much! I was having a fabulous conversation with a mom I had known prior to this event through my work. As we talked, she commented on how much she admired the sacrifices I had made for the good of my children. Honestly, until she said, "You have literally died to self for the benefit of your children," I had never really thought about it. I guess it was true in some ways. I intentionally decided that I would put the needs of my children ahead of my own. I wanted them to have all the same opportunities of children who have two parents living in the same house. I didn't want them to be without support or supervision, so I no longer did some of the hobbies I used to enjoy. I didn't want them not to excel at the sports, activities, and academics they had a passion for, so I spent almost every night of the week taking them to practices and tutors and private lessons. I didn't exactly make a conscious decision to do all this. It was one small choice after another, made out of love and guided by God.

When we look at the story of Mary washing Jesus's feet with perfume, we see an act that was sacrificial because of the cost of the perfume. But Mary did not set out to perform a sacrificial act. Mary set out to express her deep love for her Lord. And because of the love motivation, and the resulting sacrifice, Jesus proclaimed that her faith would be remembered (Mark 14:9). Everyone in the room that day found it surprising how pleasing this act was to Jesus. They openly discussed the value of the sacrifice. We don't know what acts of sacrifice motivated by our love for our children God will find pleasing. Further down the road, God will honor our acts of sacrificial love in the lives of our children and in the following generations. We will not know until eternity all who have been blessed by the sacrificial love we live every day in raising our children. It is not about the value of the sacrifice or the result we can see today. It is about living out the love we feel for our children in the ways God leads us.

I am certain that the day will come when I will be able to indulge in my hobbies again and have plenty of unscheduled time. But when my children have moved out of my house and have their own homes and families, I pray that my opportunities to express the love I have for my children and for all God's children will be plentiful! I also pray that the way I expressed my love and sacrificed for my children will influence the way they parent my grandchildren.

Greater love has no one than this, that he lay down his
life for his friends [children]. (John 15:13 NIV)

As we face this road ahead of us, knowing we are going to give all we
have for our kids, we have to be optimists! We must have the optimism
of David. As he faced challenges, he knew God was with him and that
he could count on God as the active agent in his challenging situations.
He headed into the fight with Goliath knowing that God would grant
him victory, not because of his size or strength, but because of his God.
And as much as we are facing a Goliath of a task in raising our children,
we too must know that because of the God who is with us, we can expect
victory. Additionally we need to be prepared to stand and fight for the
long haul. Remember, David took five stones. He wasn't going into the
battle assuming that God would grant him victory on the first stone. He
was ready to continue fighting for as many as five stones, not just one. We
must be that kind of optimist, knowing God will provide the victory and
being willing to fight for however long we are called upon to keep fighting.
Some days and phases are so joy filled that it feels like I have been granted
victory before I have had to throw one stone. And other days and phases
are long, and I am tired, and I feel like I have thrown so many stones that
I could not count them if I had to. In fact, in some of those stretches, it
felt like the Goliath I was fighting landed a few punches. But regardless,
we must count on God to bring about the victory in his time. Our task
is simply this—to love sacrificially, without losing so much of ourselves
that we have nothing left to give the next day. We must know that if
we continue to love our children well, and keep God's will first and our
desires behind his will, then we can count on our God to be there with
us in the fight and hand the victory to our families.

Therefore, I urge you brothers, in view of God's mercy,
to offer your bodies as living sacrifices, holy and pleasing
to God—his is your spiritual act of worship. (Romans
12:1 NIV)

We belong entirely to God. The way you live your life for God is
your offering to him. Stay focused on God and on living God's will in

your life. When you accomplish that, the best parenting will be given to your children as you seek to be exactly what God is calling you to be. After all, wouldn't God want the very best for his children? So would he lead you or direct you in a way that is not what is best for them? Keep your eyes on God and on living in his will, and you will be able to be as confident as David when he approached Goliath.

When my son was kindergarten age, a boy in his class lost his dad to cancer. A few months passed, and his mother asked if we could all go bowling to give her son a chance to talk to my son and just ask him any questions he might have. As we were getting ready to go bowling, I told my son that his friend might want to talk about missing his dad. With the simplicity of a trusting child, he said, "That's fine. I will just tell him it's no big deal—God just takes over being your dad." It is exactly that way. And with the confidence of children of God, we can face the Goliath of our day today and tomorrow, knowing that God is right there with us. We are not alone in the stands.

A Child with a Broken Heart

"Allow the children to come to me," Jesus said. "Don't forbid them, because the kingdom of heaven belongs to people like these children."

—Matthew 19:14 (CEB)

I am a teacher, having taught in public schools for thirty years. In that time, I have watched hurting children come to class and try to seem like they are doing just fine, when one look into their eyes tells me they really are not. Many of the struggles children have in school stem from a hurting heart. I talked to a counselor once who taught me the most useful phrase: "hurting people hurt people." She is so correct. It is not the well-adjusted, self-aware, at-peace-with-themselves people who cause pain in the lives of others. It is the people who are hurting who, either out of self-defense or because of anger within, cause those around them to hurt. Sadly, I have looked at far too many children who are hurting others around them because they do not have the emotional tools to manage the hurt they feel within.

In Acts 27 we read about Paul who, as a prisoner, was placed on a ship setting sail for Rome. Paul warned the crew that the journey was destined for disaster. Despite his warnings, the crew sailed on. Paul didn't really have a choice about sailing; he was a prisoner. The season made sailing dangerous, and predictably, the ship was caught in a tremendous storm. The sailors tried everything, including throwing the cargo overboard, to lighten the ship's load. Eventually the ship ran aground on a sandbar off the shore. Those who could swim had to swim to safety, and those who could not swim held on to planks and pieces of the wrecked ship to float to safety. No one perished in the shipwreck.

There are some great lessons for us in this story. I often think that single parenting feels a little like Paul must have felt when he was loaded on that ship. We really did not want to have to take this journey, did we? And we often feel like it could end in nothing but disaster. We are going to face some serious storms on our journey, and we know it. We see the season ahead, and we know there is not going to be easy sailing.

Most people who are raising children alone would not have chosen the situation for themselves. Even in the situations of those who are singled because of abuse, if they could change the person who perpetrated the abuse, they would do so to prevent themselves from parenting alone. Those who survived abuse are alone because they know that the person who abused them would not change. Raising children alone brings with it many heartaches and moments of grief that stem from how we got here. With these come our emotional struggles that result from how we got here as well. Let's face it, we are hurting and struggling as adults. And then we look at these precious children who are counting on us as *parent*, and we hope they are not hurting or struggling in the way we are. But the truth is, they are.

So here we are on our ship facing tremendous storms. We know there is no way to sail through without a shipwreck. We have to take action, but the storm is making sailing on to the destination we had originally planned impossible. So, like the crew of the ship, we need to unload the ship. We need to throw off the cargo that is weighing the ship down and seek another solution. The crew of the ship carrying Paul actually turned the ship and set the sail to run it aground, hopefully on the beach of an island. While a sandbar caught the ship and stopped it short of the beach, the crew realized they needed a solution that was not in the original plan.

Our children are hurting and grieving, and the hard fact is that we do not have the emotional tools to guide them or help them through all of the hurts, grief, and traumatic situations they have experienced. In fact, many of us do not have the emotional tools to guide ourselves through the pain we are experiencing. We must start by first recognizing that we are injured, and so are they. I have spoken to several singled people who have tried to tell me that they are "over it" and have just easily moved on. They later demonstrated through actions and words how completely false those statements were. This is the cargo we need to throw overboard to lighten the ship for sailing. We can't carry the cargo of denial and suppressed emotion on our ship. One thing we must do as parents is recognize that we need to gain tools to address our emotional damage. Too often we try to be superhuman and pretend that we are not hurt. That doesn't model a healthy approach to our children, nor does it provide our children with a healthy parent. Just toss that attitude overboard. When I was widowed, I had little to no understanding of my own grief, much less the grief my children faced. Through the help of a wonderful grief counselor, I gained understanding of my pain and slowly became capable of working through it, eventually living well beyond that place of grief. That counselor also helped me understand how vastly different the grief process was for my children. I had no idea how different the processing of emotional pain is in a child as compared to an adult. I am so thankful that she helped us through those first few years and provided us with tools for living well beyond them. I must admit that despite all those tools, there were still times when I tried to be the superhuman parent. I also must admit that there are things I regret in those past years, and as I look back, I can clearly see the hurt that motivated those actions.

While the storm raged around Paul and the crew, Paul continued to trust God and tell them God was with them and that they would survive. How out of the ordinary is this picture? A prisoner telling the crew that they will survive and that they can count on God. But Paul continued to trust God—even in this situation.

As I have raised my children, I have tried to use as many situations as possible to demonstrate for my children and teach them how they can count on God. God put wonderful professionals in my path for this situation each time it arose. And I hope I helped my children see that to count on God is to use the help he sends our way.

Understandably the first years after I was widowed were filled with a need for support from a grief specialist for me and my children. There are several ways to find this resource. Groups in churches are wonderful. An individual counselor, and even groups in an area hospital where I live, are both fantastic. God presented one counselor in particular to us, and she worked with both my children as they came to accept our situation. Additionally, she gave me tools and an understanding of what to watch for and how to recognize when my children needed more support than one loving parent could give. As my children have grown and passed through the predictable life phases, we have sought out professional support for each of them as needed. Your child's grief and hurt is not always something he or she will want to discuss or share with you. Your children may think they need to protect you from the hurt they feel. They don't want to inflict more pain on you by sharing their own pain with you. They will go through phases where they genuinely need someone else, and that does not mean you are not doing a great job as a parent.

I often think of a loving parent as the goose that laid the golden eggs from *Aesop's Fables*. We continually push ourselves to provide golden eggs of love, support, opportunities, wisdom, guidance, and care for our children. But when a child is hurting, he or she often needs a different type of egg. Our golden eggs will not suffice. There is nothing worse than trying to give a child a golden egg when what he or she really needs is a crystal one. We hurt not only ourselves but also our children when we try to be everything for them. We need to seek the help of one who can provide the crystal egg they need to see clearly and live well beyond the pain. If we try to be something we are not, we will fail. I will not provide what I am unable to provide. So trust that God has blessed others with training and wisdom to provide you with tools you need and has blessed your children with the understanding and tools they need. Follow God's leading as you are given chances to connect with trained specialists, attend groups at churches, or make use of other resources.

Just as the crew members on the ship who did not have the ability to swim had to hold on to a plank or a piece of the wrecked ship, we have to hold on to what God provides for us when our ability to swim is lacking. As the ship came apart, it provided floating planks for the nonswimmers. God puts those planks in our waters too. We need to reach out to them and hold on as we float to safety. And we need to keep hanging on to those planks until we know for certain that our feet are on the sand of the island.

Hanging on to the plank means realizing that there is not a once-and-done approach to emotional healing. With both my children, the needs resurfaced as they grew and developed and became more aware of their world and their own emotional needs. My children have a significant age gap between them. This means that they began processing the death of their father at different stages of psychological development. I started taking both of them to grief counseling with me in the beginning of our journey, and then, as the journey progressed, only one would need some work to gain tools or skills to cope with the pain. At a later time, the other would need to work to gain tools for living. This is the reality of growing and maturing children. They have psychological developmental stages that are impacted differently and at different times. Personality traits also generate different needs to address. I say all this to make this point: there is not a simple one-stop shop for the emotional healing of your child. There is not one answer that will be a solution and then you can cross "healthy well-being for my children" off your list. "Healthy well-being for my children" is something you will need to be aware of and attend to as long as you have the title of parent. Healthy well-being is something you will also need to be aware of and attend to for yourself. Feeling like you can push through when you are struggling emotionally only makes the push impossible and the emotional healing improbable.

I wanted to be the best parent I could be for my children. I didn't want them to hurt any more than they had to because they had lost their dad. But the truth is, I am human, and I can't be two people. I also hurt and struggle with the pain. I had to get help to learn how to be the best parent I could be and live well with the situation. That took help from professionals whom God placed in my life at the times when I needed them most. None of us should think we are above asking for help. We need to cry out to God daily for help, and when he sends us help in the form of support groups, counselors, and other resources, we need to be thankful to him and take the help. So often to count on God means to see the professionals whom God has put in your path to help. Don't think that calling on a God-gifted professional is something you should not do. Instead, know that God puts those people in your path to help. Grief and anger are difficult to understand at any age, especially for children, so seek the counsel of professionals.

No matter how strong the storm raged, Paul continued to profess his faith and encourage the crew. He did not let the storm, or even the shipwreck, shatter his faith. This is what we need to give our children as they begin to heal. We need to hold firm to our faith and profess that we know God will provide all the planks we need to float to safety. We need to encourage each other as we work to gain the emotional strength to hold on to the planks or learn to swim. We need to allow those who can teach us and guide us through this shipwreck of life to do what God has inspired them and blessed them with talent to do.

This shipwrecked man is the same Paul who writes, "Grace and Peace to you." He understood the immense importance of an unshakable faith and the peace that passes understanding. Our children will not have the opportunity to feel that peace unless we allow them the opportunity for healing and take those opportunities for ourselves. They can't gain the understanding of the immense value of the peace that passes understanding until they are emotionally healthy enough to experience that peace.

As a teacher, I have encountered countless numbers of students who lived the struggle of being a child with a single parent. I would hear their parents say, "Kids are resilient." No, kids are good at pretending to be resilient. They hurt, they grieve, they struggle, and they need a plank to hold on to. Don't let them pretend. Help them hold on to a plank, and get the help you need to hold on to one too. The beach is not that far away, and with the right plank, you will all make it there safely.

FACING YOUR GIANTS

And they told him, "We came to the land to which you
sent us. It flows with milk and honey, and this is its fruit.
However, the people who dwell in the land are strong,
and the cities are fortified and very large. And besides,
we saw the descendants of Anak there."

—Numbers 13:27–28 (ESV)

I have a very vivid childhood memory. This happened every night when
I was young. I would stand at the doorway of my bedroom, get my feet
in just the right position, take a deep breath, and attempt to turn off
the lights and make it into my bed in one long leap, fast enough to beat
the darkness that would allow the monsters under the bed to grab me.
It did not matter how many times I checked under the bed when the
lights were on to find only stray toys. When the darkness took over the
room, I was certain the danger under the bed appeared. And you can
place a sure bet that I was not going to check under the bed in the dark
to see if my fears were real!

Often my days as a single parent feel just like that moment right
before I flipped the lights off. I feel the monsters and giants approaching.
They feel huge and threatening and unbeatable. I am quite certain I am
not the only one who feels this. No, I am not afraid of monsters under
my bed, but the giants that rise up in my road of life are more difficult
to face than those imaginary monsters. The giants are real. While my
giants may have different names than your giants, I am sure that we all
face them. No matter what the name of the giant—loneliness, financial
concerns, exhaustion—defeat seems certain. We don't have the option
not to face our giants, though, because most of them threaten our

stability and happiness, along with our children's security and happiness now and in the future.

The current culture tries to convince us that there are things that are absolutely needed for happiness. But none of those things our culture tells us we need are God. What is absolutely needed for genuine happiness is God and being a part of the big picture of the kingdom. Yet our culture tries to tell us that what we should seek has nothing to do with that. Our culture says we should want a relationship, a spouse. We are led to seek enough sleep each night to awake feeling rested. We are told that we want financial security. But what we need is God. What we need to do is to keep our focus on the big picture of what God is doing in this world and where we are to play a role in that. This is where we start defeating our giants.

If we are focused on what God is doing and our part in it, we look at our children and realize that we are a vital part of something so much bigger than ourselves and our wants. We need to see that the moment we are in today is a part of an eternal time line. When we examine our momentary struggle from that perspective, our point on that time line looks completely different from how it appeared when the giant first stepped into view. What we are teaching our children by example and by word may be for our great-grandchild's benefit. We must train ourselves to keep our eyes focused on the big picture and the eternal time line. We need to constantly remind ourselves, *It's not about me, It's about what God wants to do in and through me.* We need to constantly ask ourselves, "What is it I am trying to accomplish?" The answer to that question disarms the giants so many times. If the answer is that I am trying to raise my children to be faith-filled and faith-directed, the giants of our culture lose power. Better still, I gain strength as I realize that what my children need to see in me and through me is the power of God working for the good in our lives. That, partnered with the perspective that we are a part of an eternal time line with a purpose to serve the good of the kingdom, is the point where we become giant-slayers! I can't tell you the number of times I have watched my children not get what I was certain they needed and then, years later, being thankful that such was the case. Whether it was my inability to pay for something they wanted that I was sure they needed, or it was one of them not making it on to a team

I was certain was vital at a specific point in their athletic development, those crisis giants that seemed unfair and undefeatable turned out to be moments when God directed the path of my children for their good further down the road. We must keep the perspective of the eternal time line and the good of the kingdom in mind.

We have several scriptural examples that can guide our thinking on this. Looking at the life of Moses in full perspective requires looking through the lens of the history of Abraham, Isaac, and Jacob leading up to the life of Moses. Moses was not one singular life but a part of an eternal time line. That time line continues on until we find the story of David, who eventually becomes king of the nation led out of slavery by Moses. We must realize that much of what God accomplishes in our lives may only be seen long after we are out of view.

Within these lives and stories of the Old Testament we see people facing giants of different labels, both literal and metaphorical. Challenges that seemed like giants, or actually were giants, can be found in these stories. Abraham faced the giant of following a promise of descendants and possession of a land that was foreign to him. He followed, despite the word from God that the fulfillment of this promise was more than four hundred years away. Isaac faced the giant of his wife not conceiving, and then twins who struggled with each other, and moving to another land during a famine. Jacob faced a giant wrestling match, eventually receiving a name change: Israel. Moses faced the giant of Pharaoh and his army, and as Moses led the nation of Israel, he faced giant struggles and enemies. And of course we recognize that David faced a giant on the battlefield.

We can relate to these as we face our own giants. Our giants exist in so many forms, and we all face them. Don't look at others and assume they do not have giants in front of them. Most likely, they do. Every one of us faces giants, and we need to remember that just as those who faced giants in scripture had God with them and the power of God to enable them, we also have God with us and are empowered by God to conquer those giants. God does not send us into our battles alone. God is with us all the time. Not only is God with us, but also he wants to empower us. We can't forget that what we are facing is the opportunity to participate in the work of the kingdom. And in that, we glorify God when we allow his strength to shine. The best way to allow God to shine through us is to allow God to empower us when we are weak. Our weakness is God's place to empower us and shine for all to see. As God empowers us to overcome our weaknesses, we learn more about the ways God has gifted us and equipped us for the challenges we are facing. We face those giants by accepting our weakness and remembering that we are not alone.

As we are facing the giants in our lives, we must also remember that while God can shine by empowering us in our weakest areas, he has also blessed us with strengths that glorify him. We need to address our giants as the people God has created us to be. We can learn so much from the encounter between David and Goliath. David is offered armor and the option to try to be something he is not. David was not a soldier trained to fight in armor; David was a shepherd who was an expert at defending his flock with a slingshot. The giant Goliath frightened the soldiers because they would have to engage in a battle up close. But David knew he would not have to get close. David knew himself and his strengths. He addressed the giant, confident in his God-given strengths. He was also aware that God was with him and that he would not go into this battle alone. Too often we attempt to tackle our giants without accepting ourselves and our strengths. We try to be something we are not and cause ourselves to struggle more than we would if we trusted who God has created us to be. We don't need to go into battle the way the giant wants us to; we need to face the battle the way God has designed us to! We can't try to wear armor that is not ours and be someone we should not be. We need to know how God has blessed us, and we must plan to use those skills and strengths. We look at what the world wants us to be, and it often leads us to try to become something we are not. And what example does that set for our children? If we return to the important question "What am I trying to accomplish?" we realize that the best person for the task in front of us is the one God created us to be.

Often when we ask ourselves the important question, we realize that the giant is not one that is really on our battlefield to begin with. Many of our giants are given a position of threat in our lives because we have lost sight of what we are trying to accomplish. If the giants seem to win the battles in your life, ask yourself if you are fighting in the manner in which you were designed by God to fight, and using the strengths you have been gifted by God to use. You also need to ask yourself if you are fighting battles God has led you to fight or battles you think you should fight because of a current cultural influence. Don't fight giants that you could walk away from, and don't wear armor that doesn't fit you to fight the giants that you genuinely need to fight. God calls us to face down the giants that threaten our family and the work we are doing in our children for the kingdom. We must be courageous and go into that battle. We have to fight and not run. We must fight those giants. We fight them because we love God and we trust the Lord to fight for us and with us.

There is an important balance that we must maintain here. We need not to become so involved in the fight that we are consumed by it. I have talked with many parents who are concerned about the social activities of their children as they move into and through their teen years. Many parents feel this is a giant that must be fought. It is, but when a parent becomes so consumed that all he or she does is fight, the relationship and trust opportunities that could be nurtured with the child become casualties. Our sacred responsibility is to love and nurture the children God has placed in our care. To spend more energy on the fight than we spend on building trust and communication with our children is counterproductive. As my children went into and through their teen years, I was blessed to have very open and honest communication with them. A part of this was based on my not becoming consumed with the battle against the giant of social pressures. The open communication made that giant powerless in our home.

Battling the giant is not all there is. God is at work building your life and your children's lives. Don't lose focus on him and what he is doing. Don't miss opportunities to teach your children about what God can do and what God will do with us and through us!

There will be many giants fought as we move through the years of raising our children. We will need to fight for our family and fight for our faith. We will have to fight against the current culture as well. But in all of it, we need to maintain the perspective of the eternal time line, on which we are a small dot. We need to remember that we are a part of work that is to glorify the kingdom.

Finally, when you are facing a giant, try to figure out where that giant comes from. I was widowed because of an accident. There was no preparation or warning. One day my husband went to work and did not come home that night. So I have feelings of abandonment. I have found that many of the giants I face come from this place. If I feel abandoned in some manner, or if I feel that my children might experience feelings of abandonment, I get battle-ready. I will often engage in an unnecessary battle or at least start picking out the rocks for my slingshot without even realizing that the giant I am preparing to take on is from a place I don't really need to fear. I imagine we all have a place like that, a place where it seems that everyone is a giant, and we should be ready to defend ourselves and our children against anyone from that place. But we must be aware of this and strive to follow God's leading when we choose to fight.

I watched a young mother at a pool one day. She had three children with her, a toddler and two older children. It did not take very long to see that she was extremely uncomfortable around water. Each time one of the older children would put his or her face in the water, she would gasp in panic. When the toddler wanted to move off the top step on to the second step, her voice became tense and louder. She must have said "Don't get water in your face" about a hundred times before she told the children that they did not know how to behave at a pool and they left. My heart hurt for her and the children because that day she was defeated by a giant, one that I am certain comes from a traumatic experience from her past. I can't help but wonder if she were given a moment to address where that giant comes from, would she face it differently? Perhaps structured swim lessons for her children so she could become more confident in their ability to swim might disarm that giant. I can't know for certain. What I do know is that some of our giants only seem big, whereas others genuinely loom over us. But none of them can claim victory over us unless we give that power to them.

> All those gathered here will know that it is not by sword or spear that the Lord saves; for the battle is the Lord's, and he will give all of you into our hands. (1 Samuel 17:47 NIV)

We can face our giants. We can look them in the eye, consider what we are trying to accomplish, and know if they are worthy of our energy to fight them. Then, with the strength we gain by keeping the perspective of God's eternal time line and seeing the big picture of the work of the kingdom of God, we can go into battle with confidence. We can face the giants, accepting who we are created to be, realizing that God can empower us in our weakness, and knowing that God is always with us. God will fight for you, with you, and through you.

You Can Call God "Daddy"

Yet to all who received him, to those who believed in
his name, he gave the right to become children of God
—John 1:12 (NIV)

Up in the mountains camping with my children in an area that
others might not find particularly beautiful or inspiring was the
perfect place for me. We were in a part of the forest that had been burned
four years before. Signs of forest fire devastation were still very visible.
Burnt tree stumps dotted the landscape, and the blackened, charred tall
trunks of the towering lodgepole pines caught the eye as they covered
the mountain slopes. But just past the most apparent signs of destruction
was another sight: green growth. Lots of green was everywhere. A thick
layer of new growth was springing up.

As I gazed on this beautiful sight, I found myself reflecting on the
handiwork of God in my children's lives. The family they once knew was
so much like the forest prior to the fire—strong, thick, vibrant, and full
of life. We had gone through our own version of a forest fire, namely,
the burn we felt as they lost their dad to death. Now, we were so much
like this area of the forest, still living with burned stumps and evidence
of the fire, but thick with new growth and potential. My children,
like this forest, are teeming with life and potential, and hope for the
future. Raising children in a single-parent home will include dealing
with children's hurts, grief, and traumatic situations. The child who
lives in a home with a missing parent consistently encounters struggles
that other children simply don't. Every time the dads' club meets at my
son's school, it is a difficult day for him. When my daughter listened to
her teenage friends complain about their dads, she was frustrated and it

caused hurt. When the camp is inviting chaperones and specifies dads to go with the boys, it is a challenge for my son. We must address these hurts and challenges and the pain that goes with them.

This also means that we need to make the most of the opportunities we encounter to show God's ability to heal and improve our situations and to bring good to us through those situations. We need to seek out the means to demonstrate to our children and teach them how to count on God. We also need to consistently emphasize and teach our children how much God loves them, values them, and treasures them. God is the parent who will not show up late or fail to support them when they are hurting. God is the parent who will not let them down.

> Sing to God, sing in praise of his name, extol him who rides on the clouds; rejoice before him—his name is the lord. A father to the fatherless, a defender of widows, is God in his holy dwelling. (Psalm 68:4–5 NIV)

The word *father* brings up different images for many people. Some people have very positive images, whereas others have images of abuse or abandonment. The fact is, no matter how hard a person tries, there is no perfect parent on earth. Every human parent is exactly that—human. And because we are human, we are inherently able to fail. For this reason, we all need to derive our image of God as a Father from scripture and spiritual experiences. We must attempt to dismiss images of God that are based in worldly experiences with specific gender and parental roles. We need to use a scripturally based focus on the unconditional and unfailing love and grace our God offers each of us as his children. Luke shows us a heavenly father who is ready to meet your needs:

> Which of you fathers, if your son asks for a fish, will give him a snake instead? Or if he asks for an egg, will give him a scorpion? If you then, though you are evil, know how to give good gifts to your children, how much more will your Father in heaven give the Holy Spirit to those who ask him! (Luke 11:11–13 NIV)

We find in scripture an explanation of God's love for us that claims us as his own children and disciplines us, helping us grow and mature in faith:

> My son, do not despise the Lord's discipline or be weary of his reproof, for the Lord reproves him who he loves, as a father the son in whom he delights. (Proverbs 3:11–12 ESV)

> And you have forgotten the exhortation that addresses you as sons: My son, do not take the Lord's discipline lightly or lose heart when you are reproved by him, for the Lord disciplines the one he loves and punishes every son he receives. (Hebrews 12:5–6 ASV)

In the book of Romans, Paul tells us that our heavenly Father loves us and does what is best for us regardless of our rebellion or even our rejection of his love:

> But God demonstrates his own love for us in this: While we were still sinners, Christ died for us. (Romans 5:8 NIV)

Later in Romans, Paul tells us of our heavenly Father who paid an excessive price to save us:

> What, then, shall we say in response to these things? If God is for us, who can be against us? He who did not spare his own Son, but gave him up for us all—how will he not also, along with him graciously give us all things? (Romans 8:31–32 NIV)

These types of scriptural references should shape our understanding of God as our Father and as the perfect Father for our children. This is a loving father who disciplines for our benefit and loves us despite our imperfect human nature. God loves us unconditionally. God not only loves us unconditionally but also loves us before we even know to love him. We are loved regardless of our sinful condition.

We love because he first loved us. (1 John 4:19 NIV)

Through scripture we can understand that our heavenly Father has claimed us as his children. We can know that we are truly children of God and can call God our Father.

The Spirit you received does not make you slaves, so that you live in fear again; rather, the Spirit you received brought about your adoption to sonship. And by him we cry, "Abba, Father." The Spirit himself testifies with our spirit that we are God's children. (Romans 8:15–16 NIV)

These scriptures provide us with some of the characteristics of our heavenly Father. Through the grace of the cross, we have unobstructed access to our heavenly Father. He never will tell you he is too busy or that what is on your heart is not important. He will not tell you that you are not a priority now and that when you need him, he will be out of town on business. More than that, he can use the difficulties in your life to your advantage.

And we know that in all things God works for the good of those who love him, who have been called according to his purpose. (Romans 8:28 NIV)

I clearly remember sitting at my late husband's funeral and praying fervently, "God, I give you these children just like Abraham gave you Isaac. I can't raise them alone, so you will have to take them." God hears our prayers. I have watched the answer to my prayer every day since then.

I have seen my children grow up with a strong sense of worth that is not consistent with what statistics say should be present. Statistics on children raised in a home where the father is absent are not encouraging. And while my children are very normal human children, they have not fallen to the struggles that statistics predict. As they grew up, I made a conscious effort to point out the times when God was there for us when we needed him. I intentionally shared with them the times that I would take my heartaches to God, and I encouraged them to do the same. When they accomplished things by using the talents God has blessed them with, I made an effort to identify how they could feel God's pleasure in the joy they were feeling. As difficult times passed and good was revealed on the other side, I would point out the work of God in providing the path for them. I tried to take every opportunity I could find to give my children the awareness of God's love, approval, provision, and hand on them.

The incredible truth is that God is the ultimate parent for each one of us. God is able to fill all the voids left by earthly parents who leave gaps in our lives by accident or by choice. It doesn't matter how much we want to be everything for our kids, we simply can't be perfect. We are human, and we are going to let them down. Whether our children have multiple parents in multiple homes or just one surviving parent in one home, the parent they need the most is God. The greatest lesson we can give them is to guide them and lead them to count on God as the parent they need the most.

I don't claim to have all the answers, and I have made more than my fair share of mistakes. But one thing I do know—God is the Father to the fatherless. God is the perfect parent to those who will accept his love. God can provide all we need in every situation and will care for us beyond our expectations if we allow him to do so. I have raised two children with only one earthly parent in their lives. The most important aspect of my approach has been to firmly teach them that they can count on God as their Father, that he will never fail them or forsake them, and that when they look to him for approval, they will always find unconditional love and grace. God is the ultimate authority telling my daughter she is lovely and the ultimate authority telling my son that he has what it takes to be a man. The most important lesson I can give my children is to teach them to count on God to provide for their needs, to count on God for perfect guidance and advice, and to look to God for approval instead of seeking the opinions of the world. I do believe that the most important lesson we can teach our children is that they can call God "Daddy."

Raising the Good Life

He has shown you O mortal, what is good. And what
does the Lord require of you? To act justly and to love
mercy and to walk humbly with your God.
—Micah 6:8 (NIV)

We live in a google culture. If you do not know something, google it and you will have an answer in seconds. If you don't like what you see, swipe left; if you like what you see, swipe right. Regardless, don't worry, because the cultural standard dictates that you don't have to commit to it or work hard at it. Just keep swiping and you can find another option instantly. The options and the answers are as plentiful as the number of people on the internet. We are saturated by options. Back in the pre-internet years, we had to research topics and work at finding information. The process of gathering knowledge on a subject took time and effort. And sometimes we still did not get the answer. Sometimes research only led us to more questions. We were limited in options by just what we could access or encounter in our local area. If our library or bookstore did not have the resources we needed, we had to wait for days for the information we wanted to be delivered. If friendships or relationships did not work out, there were only the people in our community to turn to. Our culture is vastly different now. If you want a better job, want a better apartment, want a better car, want a better church, or want a better person to date, just keep swiping, or scrolling, or googling. Somehow we think this is going to bring us the good life. If I swipe again, the next better thing will come up and I will find the good life. But in all that googling, swiping, and scrolling, we are not finding the good life. In fact, many are finding they are empty and constantly struggling with shallow friendships and relationships. What many fail to realize is that the good life is about filling the God-sized void in our hearts with God and raising our children to do the same.

In the scripture from Micah we find a simple program for living the good life. The good life is centered on doing that which is just and right, living a life filled with acts of mercy, and walking humbly with God. While the lines between right and wrong seem to shift faster than sand in a strong wind, we can find through prayer, scripture, and taking time to listen for the whispers of guidance from the Holy Spirit what is just. The honest struggle is to actually do that which is just in spite of the shifting definitions. Good scripture study can help us with this. We need to allow the words of scripture and the actions of Christ to make the definitions clear to us. When we study scripture, we need to look at more than just one short verse. We need to study the chapter and the context in which it was written. Further, we need to utilize other scriptures to clarify points of confusion within scripture. The definition of doing justly is not as difficult to discern when scripture study is approached this way. As parents, we can't stop there. We must teach our children to read, study, and know scripture in the same way.

The second part of the program is to love mercy, recognizing that loving mercy means living out acts of mercy. It's not enough to say that we love mercy. We must engage in performing and doing sacrificial acts of kindness for others. God has blessed you with children, and they need to experience your mercy toward them as well as learn from your modeling and participate with you as you demonstrate acts of mercy toward others.

The third part is that we are to walk humbly with God. *Humbly* indicates walking carefully and wisely, and most important you must walk with God. This language indicates a type of covenant. An intentional effort to walk in the direction God leads is implicit in this covenant. If we are going our own way, following our own agenda, and not maintaining an awareness of God's will for our lives, we are missing this key part of the program. It takes humility to recognize that what one wants is second to what God calls one to do. This is hard to live for ourselves and hard to teach our children. But we must teach them to seek God's will before they seek the popular way, the easier way, or the faster way. For our children who are so at ease with a google quick answer, this will be a challenge.

I know from experience that some days parenting alone can hardly feel like you are living the good life. But it really is the good life. It may seem hard and difficult and even lonely at times—but it is God's intent that we have abundant blessings and joy! Not just some joy, but abundant joy!

> And God is able to bless you abundantly, so that in all things at all times, having all that you need, you will abound in every good work. (2 Corinthians 9:8 NIV)

God does not give us a little joy or a half measure of joy—God gives in a measure pressed down and overflowing. This task we have—the task of raising the children God gave us—is one that is filled with so much joy and so much delight. We simply must choose to see that. We could spend our time looking at the struggles our children have, the days that our daughters are hormonal, or the times that our sons don't look up from the video games while we are trying to talk to them. We can focus on the never-ending pile of laundry and the ever-growing home repair list, or we can focus on the hugs and the "Thanks, Mom" moments. I need to focus on the beautiful leaf my toddler was determined to give me every morning as school started in the fall—yes, I have a thirteen-year-old leaf in the center console of my car to remind me of those fantastic joy-filled moments. Those are the beautiful joy-filled moments that are the abundant life God is giving us. Keep your eyes focused on the fall leafs, the hugs, and the "Thanks, Mom" pictures. These are the total joy-filled items that are the full measure pressed down and overflowing!

For many, there is a need to know what this looks like on a day-to-day basis. What is it to actually live the good life? It looks like everyone going to the grocery store together to share the chore and sometimes having to stop your kids from fighting in the middle of the store. And then when you get home, everyone works together to get the groceries unloaded from the car and into the kitchen. It looks like a family sitting down to dinner together and laughing because Mom burned the food again and it tastes awful. In such a scenario, I am laughing with my children because I am not trying to be the perfect cook. It looks like everyone going to church together to worship, even if one of the family members doesn't want to go. Everyone gets to go anyway! The good life is full of mishaps and missteps, but there is a lot of laughter in most of those moments. The good life involves mission work for the church and others in our community. It looks like cleaning out closets and taking outgrown clothes to the local agency for those struggling. These heartwarming visuals stem from doing what is just and right, extending mercy, or exercising humility while intentionally seeking God.

Every year when I start to put up our Christmas tree, I watch my favorite movie. My children don't enjoy the movie. In fact, they openly groan and complain as I load the DVD into the player and start it. But no Christmas season is complete without a viewing of *It's a Wonderful Life* in our house. Perhaps when my children are older they will start to recognize more of why I love this movie. I love the message that a single person living a simple life, doing what is just and right, extending mercy to his neighbors, and following where he knows he is called to follow, even if it is not where he wants to go, has a profound and positive effect on an entire community. That is what I call living the good life! He almost doesn't see it. That is exactly where so many of us are in our lives. We go through our daily lives and we don't see that we are impacting our children and our community. We may never get to know what differences we are making. But we can't afford to be blind to the good life we are living. We need to see the amazing life in a smile and in a simple thank-you from our children. We need to soak in the joy in their laughter because soon they will be grown and living in their own homes, and that laughter will be a memory we will want to have treasured. We need to remember that even on the hardest days, when we are absolutely exhausted and feeling defeated, the good life is right in front of us. While the road seems long and lonely, you will find yourself at the turning point much sooner than you realize. Those precious children will have grown up, and you will realize that you have been living the good life.

Do Justly

He has told you O Man what is good; and what does the Lord require of you but to do justice, and to love kindness, and to walk humbly with your God?

—Micah 6:8 (MEV)

In the years raising my children, I have sat through countless hours of swim lessons, diving lessons, softball practices, baseball practices, soccer practices, track practices, basketball practices, singing recitals, piano lessons, karate classes, private karate lessons, math tutoring, and flag football practices—and I am sure I have missed something. Then there were the games, meets, and contests. I know my personal social life would be in better shape and my physical fitness would be better too if I had spent that much time on myself, or if I'd had someone to split that time with, but such wasn't the case. So I did what I thought was right. I made the choices I felt led to make. I chose what I believed was best for my children and our family. The guiding scripture that defines the good life begins with "Do justly." That means to try to do what is just and right. That is not as easy as we hope it would be. As much as we study the life and teachings of Christ, our human condition still gets in the way. We function out of emotion, pride, jealousy, or fatigue, and at times we fail to do the right thing. But our striving should be to know what is right and to do that as often as humanly possible. And we should be striving to teach our children to do the same.

When my daughter was in middle school, she ran on the cross-country team. She worked all season long to get her time fast enough to run for the A team. Finally, at the last meet of the season, she earned her place on the top team for the meet. Race day came, and of course

I was there to cheer her on. The race began, and she got off to a good start. In cross-country meets the spectators can't see the entire race. The girls soon disappeared out of view, and I quickly made my way to where they would come back into the clearing so I would be able to see her and cheer for her. Soon the leaders came into the clearing, followed by the other racers. But my daughter was not in sight. I couldn't figure out where she was or why she was missing. After most of the racers had passed, she finally emerged into the clearing, running fast and strong, far too fast to be as far behind as she was. When she finished the race, I met her at the line and asked what happened. She told me that one of her teammates had fallen and that she had stopped to help her. I didn't even let her finish telling me the rest of the story. I interrupted her and began a lecture about competition and racing and doing her best, and then I heard myself. I was embarrassed by what I was saying. I apologized to my daughter over and over and told her as many times as I could that she had done the right thing and that I was wrong. Later we found out that the teammate had fallen on account of a serious medical condition and that she needed someone to help her and get her medical attention. If my daughter had not done the right thing that day, her teammate may have suffered serious or critical injury.

We are not always going to make the right choice, but we can make the right choice in how we respond when we recognize what we have done. And we can acknowledge our children when we see them make the just and right choice, encouraging them to continue on that path.

In 1 Samuel, chapter 1, we read of Hannah, who longs for a child. When Samuel is born she cares for him until he is weaned. Then she takes him to the temple and gives him to the Lord. This is just one of the scriptural stories where a parent recognizes the need to put her child in God's hands. I think this is the perspective we need to have as single parents. We need to allow God to parent our children. When our children are in his hands, good can be made for them where bad might be intended. The success they experience will be for his glory and part of the work of the kingdom. And it will be clearer to them what is just and right because God will reign in their hearts. I have watched as both my children have responded to situations and challenges with actions that are just and right, when out of mommy protectiveness or mommy pride, I would have had a different and less just response. I have worked to pray with my children, teach my children scripture, and then let God reign in their hearts and minds. I am certain the just and right responses of my children are because of the leading of their heavenly Father. I am so thankful for a loving God who teaches them so much more about the good life than I can demonstrate.

So while my reaction at the finish line was not the just and right reaction, I did do the just and right thing by apologizing. I also had done what was right by my daughter by simply being present. While raising my children, I was present at all of those practices, performances, and competitions. This is one of the just and right choices we as single parents must make. We must choose to make sacrifices so our children can be who God designed them to be. This means listening to them when they voice an interest in something and also supporting them as they learn and attempt the things they think interest them. I remember several attempts at hobbies and activities that were not successful. But we explored them because my child had an interest. I will confess to presenting the things I hoped they would want to do, but those were eliminated almost immediately. I learned that my children were going to show me where their hearts led them, not go where I wanted to see them go. Ballet and baseball did not last very long in my house.

What is just and right is to let who God created them to be shine. Additionally, take time to learn about what shines from them because that is a God-given talent and passion. My daughter found a place to help children in our community through martial arts. I had absolutely no knowledge of martial arts prior to her interest in this area. But I watched and learned and supported her. I cried tears of joy every time she broke boards and was thrilled beyond words as she moved confidently through the ranks. She now has a lifelong skill set that otherwise, if I had not chosen to do what was just and right, if I had denied her the opportunity to study martial arts because I didn't know enough about it, she would have missed. Further, I can't know the impact she may have had on the children she worked with in the community who came to learn while she was helping teach classes. She may have impacted a life that we will never know about—but God knew and led her there. I have heard parents say, "My child was interested in that, but I just didn't see why we should." We need to make sacrifices of time and energy to support what God plants in our children's hearts. It is not about what we want or understand. Rather, it is about what God is doing in their lives.

It is also important that we be there for our children to demonstrate how to show support and teach them to support each other as well. This is part of doing what is just and right. My son sat through belt tests and tournaments, and my daughter sat through soccer games, football games, and basketball games. My son is not a fan of martial arts, and my daughter is not really a sports fan. But they were always there for each other. After my daughter was grown and living in her own apartment in another town and my son had an important game, she would make the effort to be there for him, not because she was a sports fan, but because it was the right thing to do for her brother.

If we parents consistently live out what is just and right as best we can, our children will learn the heart-deep value of living that way. I have taught public school choir for thirty years. Most of my students will be in choir for three years during the time they are in middle school. It is heartbreaking to know of the large number of students who are gifted singers who will go through three years of choir and never have a parent attend a performance. Understandably, some of these parents are working or unable to attend on occasion, but for a parent to miss every performance for three years is unbelievable and truly heartbreaking. You tell your children something by being present. By watching them do the thing that matters to them, you are doing the just and right thing.

As I look back, I see how God blessed me with some very valuable gifts in all those hours spent watching. Most importantly, I showed my children I believe in them. When you are the only parent able to be present, your children need you there believing in them. And if the other parent is present, your children still need you there believing in them. Two parents can be there believing in them. How fantastic for your child to have multiple parents believing in them. Keep the focus on showing your child you support him or her. That is what is just and right.

Another blessing I gained from all those hours of practices, performances, and games was some valuable one-on-one time with the child who was not in action. Too often, the demands on a single parent's time are steep. Conversations and moments of one-on-one time that are otherwise rare can happen during the hours of watching. I quickly realized that while I was supporting the interest of one child, I could afford to give one-on-one attention to the other. Some wonderful walks and talks happened with my daughter while my son was on the soccer field. I learned all the names my son had given each toy train while my daughter worked on her martial arts skills. If I had been home, I would not have grasped those moments because I would have been rushing around the house trying to accomplish all of the necessary household tasks that overload all of us. Those one-on-one moments are among the things that are just and right for our children. Additionally, my children learned to be flexible and complete homework or other tasks while on bleachers or in a car. Sometimes what is right leads us to gain a valuable life skill, like learning to get tasks done no matter where we are. The perfect setting for a task may not materialize. The lessons of flexibility have been a great benefit to both my children.

The most valuable result of doing the right thing for my children, regardless of the impact on my time, has been realized as they have gotten older. Watching the way they care about what matters to each other is priceless. The just and right way to treat one another builds on the attitude of "if it is important to you, then it is important to me because you are important to me." Supporting each other is just and right. The amazing relationship my children share is overflowing with support for each other and for what matters to each of them. Seeing that flourish is the good life!

Doing what is just and right is not simple and easy. It takes listening to God and following his will for our lives and our children. Sacrifice of time and energy is always going to be a part of doing what is right. I know that I have missed out on all sorts of "girls' nights" and other social opportunities. But someday, far too soon, I will have all the time to myself I want. I am going to miss the times spent doing homework on the bleachers. I am going to miss learning new things because my children bring such things into my world. I am going to miss the amazing conversations that happen in the car while I am driving. Many of those conversations gave me the opportunity to discuss with my children what is just and right in so many areas of life. I am genuinely going to miss those talks. I treasure every hour spent as I tried my best to do what was right for my children and as I tried to teach them what was just and right. I am going to miss hearing, "Mom, did you see when I …?" That is the good life.

The type of family that supports each other and expects the best from each other doesn't happen automatically. There are some fundamental family practices that will nurture the instinct to do what is just and right, as follows:

- Pray together. Pray often, and give every member of the family a chance to participate in voicing praises and lifting concerns. Teach each of your children to listen to the others' prayers. This is valuable time as it helping them bring what is important to them to God and giving them the opportunity to hear what matters to each family member.

- Remind your children often that if something is important to someone they love, then it is important to them. Help them learn how to work as a family unit for the good of all of the members. This includes helping with dishes and basic household tasks. Give a list of what needs to be accomplished, and divide the tasks to be done so the whole family accomplishes all that is needed while working together. Hold each family member accountable for their part in the family team. Children benefit from responsibilities and need to be held accountable for accomplishing them. This will help them understand that there are times when we have to do what is right, not what we want. That will be a valuable tool for them throughout life and a guiding force in helping them do what is right when they are adults and no one is around to hold them accountable.

- Teach your children to be loyal to each other. It is normal for teens to become annoyed with younger siblings. But teach them loyalty to each other. They don't need to disrespect their siblings. Children need to be taught that they can damage that relationship. Damaging the relationship between siblings simply must not be acceptable in the family. That is not what is just and right. Certainly the usual arguments will happen, but these need to be handled by teaching your children to try to see things from the other person's perspective. Most importantly they need to be taught to respond in a way that is just and right, not angry and spiteful. There will be times when you think you may need a whistle, but referee with love and authority, and teach them to be loyal.

- Teach your children boundaries, and tell them that boundaries are love. That's why God gives them to us too. Put boundaries in place that keep them in the just and right zones of life, and then enforce them. How can we expect children to do what is just and right if we do not define the boundaries and keep them definite and clear? Children will want the boundaries to move, and they will push and make all kinds of efforts to move them. But as parents, we have a responsibility to do what is just and right for our children. Having fluid boundaries that are not enforced and cause our children to question what is actually just and right is not parenting in a manner that is just and right. Love your children well by establishing and enforcing just and right boundaries.

- Teach your children sympathy and empathy for others. When the arguments are happening between siblings and you ask them to see things from the other person's perspective, you start this. Seek opportunities to serve others through your church and in your community. Consistently offer your children the perspective of others. Show them through service opportunities that no matter how difficult your situation may seem, there is someone with a circumstance as challenging or worse. There are so many benefits to this practice. Not only will your children learn to use sympathy and empathy as a guide for what is the just and right thing to do, but also they will learn to be grateful for all the blessings they do have. It is hard to feel poorly about yourself or to indulge in self-pity when you are serving others. Both you and your children will gain so much from the emphasis of sympathy and empathy in your responses to others. The clarity of what is just and right that results is the greatest benefit of all.

It may seem like the opposite of the good life when you are making sacrifices of time, energy, and resources to support your children's interests and be present for them. It may not feel like the good life when you are enforcing boundaries and your children are pushing back. I assure you, there have been many times when I felt like I was losing the battle for the good life. Now as I look back, I am thankful and filled with joy. I am blessed by having done what I believed was just and right for my children. This really is the good life!

LOVE MERCY

He has shown you, O mortal, what is good. And what does the Lord require of you? To act justly and to love mercy and to walk humbly with your God.

—Micah 6:8 (NIV)

My son had played an entire soccer game on a hot day. Loaded in the car and heading home, he was about to open a fresh cold bottle of water when he saw a homeless man on the sidewalk at a stoplight. Without hesitation he asked to roll down the window and give the man his water bottle. I can't remember what the score of the soccer game was, but I know that day involved a victory.

The good life is a life that demonstrates mercy to the level that the person showing mercy is described as one who loves mercy. Loving mercy means living out acts of mercy—acting merciful, performing acts of mercy, and doing sacrificial acts of kindness for others. God has blessed you with children, and they need to experience your mercy toward them as well as learn from your modeling and participate with you as you demonstrate acts of mercy toward others.

One starting point for demonstrating mercy to your children is to support them with your presence and let what is important to them become important to you. That was a significant discussion in the last chapter, but it is important to recognize that the sacrificial act of support for your children is a strong foundation you can use to imprint mercy on their hearts.

Mercy begins with grace and forgiveness. Teach your children grace and forgiveness by extending it to them when they need it. If you are not able to extend forgiveness and grace to your children, they will not learn to do the same for others. It is important that when your children make mistakes, you hold them accountable and allow them to face consequences. This is actually the first step in showing them grace and forgiveness. After the resurrection, Jesus allows Peter to answer, "Yes, Lord, you know I love you" three times (John 21:15–17). Peter had denied Christ three times and was now making things right from his own perspective with Jesus. When we hold our children accountable and allow them to face consequences, we also allow them the opportunity to set themselves in a position to receive grace and forgiveness. Then, once we have held them accountable, we must give them the genuine experience of grace and forgiveness from a parent who loves them. When my children failed to meet expectations, they knew without a doubt that there would be consequences. When their teachers had a reason to contact me, even those teachers knew that my children would face consequences. But at the same time my children always knew that they were loved and valued and would be forgiven.

Another component of this is learning to ask them for forgiveness when we are wrong. I shared the story of my error at the finish line of my daughter's cross-country meet. I asked for forgiveness from her and gave her the opportunity to extend grace and forgiveness as well. It is a wonderful gift we can give our children when we allow them to extend forgiveness and grace. They will learn the joy of forgiving and the freedom they gain when they forgive. As parents, we also need to make sure that our children know that God is so much better at grace and forgiveness than we will ever be.

Engage in acts of mercy with your children, and affirm their ideas and desires in this area. When my daughter was in grade school, she listened to a sermon at church about meeting the needs of those in our community. She came home with an idea for her upcoming birthday party. She wanted to have a birthday party centered on a food drive for the local food pantry. I was so thankful that my daughter wanted to do something like this. Supporting this idea was a blessing and a great way to foster a love of mercy. I contacted the food pantry and received a list of the most-needed items. We asked party guests to gather and bring as many items in each category as possible. Her birthday party was spent stocking the shelves of the food pantry with three vans worth of items.

That type of birthday party was a great way to celebrate her growing sense of mercy.

As parents we can't wait for our children to gain inspiration to do service on their own. We need to teach and instill this behavior through action and attention. Small things like prompting your children to open a door and hold it open, carry a package for someone who has very full hands, or offer to help when they see someone who needs help are moments of prompting your children to action that need to be complemented by your children watching you do the same types of acts for others. One of the most amazing examples of this I have witnessed was performed by a complete stranger. I was in the midst of a huge rockscaping project in my yard. This was the type of project that involved several days of work and borrowing a tractor from a friend. I was trying to move tons of rock before another load of rock would be delivered the next day. I was working as the sun was setting, and a car stopped in front of my house. A young boy stepped out of the car, and his mom, who was driving the car, got out on her side. The boy offered to help with a few loads of rocks. This incredible young man saw a woman working alone on a huge project and just wanted to do something to help. What an awesome demonstration of living out what it is to love mercy. His mom was also incredible to stop and willingly support him in his desire to help others. This would require her to go out of her way and alter her schedule to wait while he helped. If I were the parent driving, I may not have been as supportive and willing to put my agenda aside and support my child as he or she felt prompted to act out the mercy we are called to live. This is the challenge to us as parents: watch for the times when we need to prompt our children, and support the times when they feel prompted by their heavenly Father.

Another key component to living out a love of mercy is selflessness. We need to cultivate selflessness in our children because it is not a natural component of the human condition. We naturally want to serve ourselves and our own ambitions. We have to purposefully seek to live out our discipleship and put the claim of Christ ahead of our natural tendency to serve ourselves. We need to use as many opportunities as we can to teach and model this to our children.

> Blessed are those who hunger and thirst for righteousness, for they will be filled. (Matthew 5:6 NIV)

We cannot be filled with righteousness if we are filled with self. We are called by our faith to be disciples and let our self-concerns be replaced by fruits of the Spirit.

> But the fruit of the Spirit is love, joy, peace, forbearance, kindness, goodness, faithfulness, gentleness, and self-control. Against such things there is no law. (Galatians 5:22–23 NIV)

We need to make certain that we model selfless discipleship for our children. We also need to make certain that when we see them act out of discipleship, we recognize their action and affirm them. Discipleship is challenging because we need to be willing to follow where Jesus leads. The call of the first disciples while they were fishing is an example of that. Jesus said "Follow me," and they did. They did not ask where or for what type of pay. They did not ask about the benefits package or the opportunities for advancement. This type of willingness to follow Christ is a challenge for us in our self-directed goal-oriented society. But it is the one goal we should be striving for. The disciples did not ask Jesus where he was going; they simply followed. The more we simply follow, the stronger our relationship with Christ becomes. A stronger relationship leaves less room for selfishness and cultivates our selfless responses to those in need of mercy.

Discipleship also means doing the task we are called to do regardless of our desires. Often we don't desire to serve and give selflessly. But this is what we are called to do as disciples, and it is a part of the good life formula. We need to remember that not everyone is blessed with the same talents and skills. Further, we would not be an effective body of Christ if we were all called to perform the same acts of mercy. There is a wide variety of the types of merciful acts needed, and we must be willing, like that impressive young boy, to move rocks if that is what is placed in front of us to do. God has blessed us and will call us at various times for various acts.

Sometimes it is moving rocks, and sometimes it is filling a food pantry. God calls and informs you of your task; agree to go, or support your children when they hear the call and agree to go. God will give you and your children the needed skills and attitude required for the merciful act. We have to let go of our plans and schedules and be willing, like the mom who was willing to stop at my home and wait while her incredible son moved rocks for a stranger. That is the act of a disciple who is selflessly following the lead of Christ. The truth is that we worry about our plans. We are concerned about sticking to the agenda and schedule we have set for ourselves. Yet, when we follow in discipleship and perform the acts of mercy God presents to us, God provides us what we need and surrounds us with people who will help us and support us. Our schedules will work out, and the plans we have will either become less important or be fulfilled.

Engaging in acts of mercy, living out compassion and kindness, and following in discipleship seems like a daunting task for us as adults and seems like an impossibility for our children. But it is not that difficult. It means following where we are led and watching out for those around us who need us to give them our energy and time. The honest truth is, we will be happier, and so will our children, when we live out a life that loves mercy. Watching my daughter fill shelves at a food pantry, looking into the kind eyes of a young man who stops to help move rocks, watching my son give away his cold fresh water after a hot soccer game—these are elements of the good life.

WALK HUMBLY WITH YOUR GOD

He has shown you, O Man, what is good. What does
Yahweh require of you, but to act justly, to love mercy,
and to walk humbly with your God?

—Micah 6:8 (WEB)

"Walk humbly with your God" is a five-word phrase that has immense
meaning. It covers more than a humble attitude. It also addresses
the idea that we will walk with God. We will seek God first and strive
to walk in his will, in a covenant relationship. This indicates daily effort
in walking carefully and wisely to maintain our relationship with God.
That involves scripture study, prayer time, quiet time, and worship. It
also requires that we recognize and value the strength and goodness of
God, not misguidedly treasure our own strengths and talents. We also
need to recognize that we have weaknesses and a tremendous need for
grace. In addition, we must realize that our children have weaknesses
and a tremendous need for grace.

It is a part of our culture to value those who appear to be the
winners. We value excellence and need to be aware of the possibility
that we might confuse the value of excellence with personal worth.
Our worth comes from our position as children of God, not from our
accomplishments. If we get these two things confused, we will struggle
to maintain our humble attitude. Without humility, we will struggle to
recognize our need for God to guide and direct our daily living. The
exciting news for us is this: God loves us and values us regardless of our
perceived excellence in this world, and he wants us to walk with him
every day.

I remember the first night I had my newborn daughter at home. I looked at that precious baby sleeping and was overwhelmed with love. We love our children with a depth that words can't describe. That love becomes a part of our existence, and we don't even realize the intensity. That love is a vital part of being a parent. It motivates our willingness to make sacrifices for our children. That love also is the source of parental pride. Humility can be tricky when parental pride rises up. We have to monitor within ourselves what is it that is motivating us to push and promote our children. Is our motivation our love, which will embrace everything that is good for them, even the difficult and challenging things, or is it our pride, wanting our children to only experience victory, causing others to wonder who is most proud of the victory they won?

When my son played his first high school football game, the opposing team was from a very strong program in the area. Their reputation was accurate. I honestly don't remember the score, except that it was a lot of points to zero. After the game, my son and his friends gathered, and we parents all took a picture of our boys to document the first high school football game. That evening one of the parents taking pictures posted the photo on social media and included the extremely lopsided losing score. One of the comments on the post reflected amazement about the parent posting about a loss. Parental pride and parental love are different. We need to realize that parental pride is not a foundation for walking humbly. Parental love is a foundation for walking humbly and for teaching our children that our value does not depend on earthly accomplishments. Additionally, we can be blinded by parental pride to push or promote our children in directions that may not be where God would lead them—or us. Humility is a challenge, but it is a necessity for those of us seeking to walk in God's will for our own lives and for the way in which we guide our children to seek God's will for their lives.

The first time I really saw this show up in my parenting was when my daughter started dance. She was kindergarten age and started dance for the first time. After only one class, the instructor moved her from the beginning-level class to the next level up. I was so proud! I could not wait for the first recital. My daughter did not have the same reaction. She did not like dance. She was not having fun and did not feel any excitement toward dance. She only wanted to be in dance because her friend was taking dance too. But her friend did not get moved up from the beginning class. Without her friend, my daughter discovered that dance held no fun or joy. I was so puffed up with pride over her talent that I didn't listen to what she was telling me. By the time the first recital came, she was ready to quit. As soon as the first recital was complete, she did quit. I learned a lot from that adventure in dance. Please don't think I am saying we should not be proud of our children. We are going to be proud of them, and that is normal. But when we lose the ability to walk humbly with God, when we fail to seek what will bring joy to our children or will keep them in God's will, we need to rein in that pride.

As we keep the parental pride in check, we need to recognize that some of the time when we are "protecting" our children from emotional pain, we are really protecting ourselves from a blow to our parental pride. This is seen in the "everyone is a winner" approach. Studies have shown that the participation award approach only diminishes the meaning and value of accomplishment and serves to generate lower self-esteem in our children. Do we really think our children are not going to be capable of learning and growing from a loss? Do we really think our children will be permanently damaged by a losing score in a recreational league game? Or is our parental pride too fragile to deal with a loss? I know from experience that my children have learned more and gained more emotional strength from the setbacks and failures they encountered. And what about those sports contests where the approach is not to keep score? After every one of those, my children could tell me exactly what the score was and what team won. If I focused on helping them learn how to improve and helping them grow emotionally from the event, they did not seem damaged by a loss. When I focused on helping them graciously accept defeat and react in a sportsmanlike manner, I believe they actually gained more from the loss than they would have gained from a win. Additionally, if I worked to find what God could teach them and teach me in the event, healthy parental pride remained unscathed, and the unhealthy parental pride was absent. Clearly present at those times was the unconditional love I feel for my children. My love was evident to them as I worked to help them see what God was doing and how we could walk humbly with God through the event.

It is hard to keep the parental pride out of the equation. I have had so many moments when I wanted to plaster pictures and captions of my amazing kids all over social media and tell the whole world how incredible they are! But that is not going to further my humble walk with God, and it will not teach or model a humble walk with God for them. How can we help our children discern where God is leading them if we are blinded by pride? We all love our children, and we all have parental pride. More importantly, we all have the responsibility to teach our children to walk humbly with God—in the direction of God's will for them.

Sorting out God's will for ourselves is challenging and difficult. We need to approach the matter prayerfully and with an open willing heart, straining to listen to the subtle whispers of the Holy Spirit. I have found that parental pride can make it impossible to sort out where God is leading my children. If I am teaching my children to walk humbly with God, then I will have to keep my parental pride out of the way. Part of keeping the parental pride out of the way is keeping a focus on my children's dreams and aspirations. When I became prideful over my daughter's success in dance, I did not remain focused on what desire had led her to the dance class. Nothing in my parental pride supported the desire she held in her heart about going into the class.

No matter how much parental pride flourishes as we watch our children accomplish something that fits into our dreams for them, it is meaningless if it is not what God leads them to dream. When we remove our pride, we make room for the dreams of our children. Often God will put passions in their hearts we would never imagine. Walk humbly with God, and watch as he nurtures dreams and aspirations in your children you would not imagine.

Keeping pride in check to walk humbly with God is not restricted to hobbies and activities. It applies to every aspect of your children's daily walk. Our humble approach will allow us parents to support them even in areas of struggle. As my children have reached higher levels in school, particularly in math, my weakness in this area became more obvious. Humility, combined with a significant lack of math aptitude, made it clear to me that the best way to support my oldest child's education was through math tutors and strong math teachers. Pride would have stopped me from seeking the teaching he needed to be successful. Walking humbly means recognizing the people God sends into our children's lives. Blessings of people who would teach my son to swing a baseball bat or help my daughter with calculus could have been missed if pride had prevented me from admitting the need.

Walking humbly means recognizing our own limitations as parents and not allowing these to limit our children. At times we as parents will need to educate ourselves about the things that matter to our children. We must not let pride limit the opportunities our children have. As a teacher of choral music, I have had several parents tell me that they were reluctant to allow their children to sing in the choir because they did not sing themselves or know anything about singing. I understand that reluctance. But some of the most talented singers I have had the opportunity to teach were children of parents who did not consider themselves singers. We need to be humble enough to allow God to lead our children into what God had in mind when he created them. We should not let pride limit our children's opportunities. Be humble enough to admit your lack of knowledge in the areas that capture your children's aspirations.

Another aspect of walking humbly with God is recognizing our children's challenges and supporting them in addressing and overcoming these challenges. Entire books can be written on this topic. I will not attempt to present myself an expert on the challenges that many children face. Our children face learning differences, physical and psychological differences, health challenges, and nutritional sensitivities and allergies. The list can go on. In my years as a teacher, I have seen prideful responses where parents did not want to accept that their children had challenges and refused to learn about those challenges or seek support for their children. I have also seen parents who humbly accepted their limited knowledge and sought solutions and support for their children while striving to learn as much as they could about the challenges their children faced. Our children need us to approach their needs with humility and a willingness to educate ourselves in areas where we lack knowledge. A humble response will provide your children with the support they need and will model to them how to address challenges. Sometimes as we educate ourselves we learn that we need to advocate for our children. This also requires humility as we step into situations in which we are not experts and try to gain what is best for our children.

My son has dyslexia. The first time I attended a meeting to establish accommodations for his education, I felt extremely uncertain. I had learned all I could, had sought the advice of other professionals and reading specialists, and had done all I could to prepare and educate myself. The irony is that as an educator, I attended these meetings as a teacher regularly. Now, as a parent, I felt completely uneasy and incapable of advocating for my own child. Regardless of the feelings of incompetence, I needed to humble myself and take risks to do what my child needed me to accomplish. Over the years, I gained knowledge and strength in my ability to advocate for my child. We can accomplish far more than we realize, but it starts at the point of humility and recognition of our need to learn.

Humility is also demonstrated when we are willing to be human. How many times have we told our kids, "You learn more from your losses and mistakes than from your victories"? Yet we try to pull off the perfect superhero parent act all the time. We make the best cookies, volunteer at every opportunity, cook, clean, maintain the house, manage the budget, fix the car, mow the yard, do the laundry, help with homework, drive to practices, take pictures at the games, post them on social media, scrapbook, maintain the family calendar, keep an eye on the friends they choose, and yes, work a full-time job! In all of this, we try to produce a perfect world for our kids. Perhaps this isn't the very best we can offer our kids. Maybe we can go out on a limb and offer them something to learn from—allow them to know our mistakes and see when we are frustrated or exhausted. We must demonstrate to them the courage to be humble and vulnerable. We need to honestly allow our children to see our weak points.

I don't bake the best cookies. I bake cookies from frozen batter. In fact, I have openly and honestly let my children know that I am not a good cook. If you were to ask them, they would quickly tell you that cooking is not something I accomplish well. That is not an insult; it is reality for my kids—and humility for me. I haven't created the perfect world for my children. I have done the best I can with God's help, but I am human and humble.

I won't ever forget the day the power went out at the house. I figured it was the result of storms that had recently gone through. Then after a few hours, I checked with the neighbors, only to find that I was the only one in the area with the power out. Still, I couldn't figure out why my power was out. Finally I called the power company. I was mortified when I was told that I had forgotten to pay the bill. The reminder note had not made it to my house in the mail—our mail delivery person is not perfect either—and I did not get the disconnect notice. The truth is that I was too busy and just forgot to pay the bill. I didn't have to tell my children the truth—but they will learn more about the importance of staying organized from this than from any of my countless lectures. They will learn more about the importance of fiscal responsibility from this than from any of my budget lessons. Hearing the voice of my teen son responding to my confession with my own words—"You need to keep things organized so you can keep track of things"—was bittersweet. I couldn't have taught it better than through humble honesty.

Another moment of humility happened the day when my "superhero parent" persona snapped. I came home from work to find that the dog, who was not on board with his new diet, had gotten into the kitchen trash. He was looking for a snack, I have no doubt. What he found was the trigger to an emotional outburst. I simply couldn't take one more stick on my load. I broke, yelling at the dog as he scampered out the back door into the yard and sitting down on the floor among all the trash crying. Usually I strive not to let my children see me break down. I save that for nights when I am unable to sleep. But that day, I broke. I ranted at the dog and cried. I cried hard! As I got up to go get a trash bag and start cleaning up, I came face-to-face with my teenaged son. He put his hands on my shoulders and said, "I'll clean this up. And, Mom, it's going to be okay." Then he hugged me. In that moment he demonstrated maturity, responsibility, willingness to move to action, compassion, emotional strength, and faith that God will provide. Besides an opportunity to see some amazing qualities shine in my son, allowing my human frailty to show in front of him accomplished more. It gave me the chance to model humbleness. It gave me a chance to model accepting help when I needed it. And it gave me a chance to honestly tell him that he was right, that it was going to be okay because God is with us. I was having a really difficult moment, but I was able to affirm my child's compassionate and faith-filled response. I was able to say, "I am so proud of you and so

51

thankful for who you are." If I couldn't be humble, then I wouldn't have been able to say, "You are so right." I would have missed an opportunity to affirm those characteristics that matter so much.

Walking humbly also enabled me to take the help with the trash the dog had scattered. I didn't need to try to get up and be "superhero mom." I took the help. Walking humbly is being willing to say to someone who offers help, "Thank you." God will send us people who are capable and willing to help us at the times we need help. We need to be humble to see the people whom God has placed around us who will step in and help us when we need it. And we need to be humble and accept the help those people offer. There is a term, "wingman," that I learned watching movies decades ago. The term refers to the pilot of the aircraft flying slightly behind and beside the lead jet. As I understand from my movie-watching education, there is great advantage to a good wingman. We can't let pride cause us to think we don't need a wingman. Be humble so you don't underestimate the importance of your wingman. God provides the wingman you need for every flight. Accept the help from others. It not only gives you the help you need, but also it models for your children that parents need more than themselves. They learn to remain humble, to accept help, and most importantly to know that only God is omnipotent.

We parents need to realize that the way we respond to situations and life's complications teaches so much more to our children than anything we say. The humble walking with God is not only for our happiness and quality of life; it is also to model for our children how they too can live a genuinely good life. Our effort to walk humbly with God accomplishes this vital modeling for our children. We model for them what humility looks like, we show them humility, and we show them that we recognize that God will show up and provide what we need every time we have a need. We show them how to trust the path God leads us to walk instead of the road we would choose. We show them how to recognize personal limitations without condemnation and how to be grateful for our talents, not prideful.

Through experience with far too many attempts at being the superhero parent, I have come to understand that not only do I set myself up to become overwhelmed and fail, but also this provides hurtful modeling for my children. It is not healthy for children to think that a parent never fails, never has limitations, and will always be perfectly executing life every day. Not only does this cause them to have a completely unrealistic view of who you are, but also it sets them up for unrealistic expectations of themselves when they are parents and establishes an unrealistic grasp of reality. Reality is sometimes a struggle—it's not always happy family game night and a perfect meal. Sometimes its laundry, too many bills to pay, and it-was-a-hard-day-at-work night. Kids don't need to suffer because of reality, but they don't need delusion either.

A parent who always pays undivided attention to their children, provides regular family game time and an endless list of fun adventures is not a healthy model. If your child is raised by the perfect superhero parent, when he or she grows into adulthood, he or she will have a very unrealistic expectation of relationships and parenting. When your children become parents and have had a hard day at work and don't manage a happy smile and the perfect meal, or don't receive it from their partner, they will not understand that reality. That is a recipe for broken relationships. We need to express our struggles and let our children see that we can love each other on it-was-a-hard-day-at-work nights. When as adults they can't get the laundry, cleaning, cooking, and shopping done, or get the bills paid, the yard work done, and all the demands of reality met while maintaining the ideal of 100 percent undivided attention to their children, they will perceive themselves to be failed parents. Don't establish a dangerous ideal for your children. Provide love for your children, but also provide humble reality.

The reality is that sometimes I need help and can't accomplish everything life demands. Walking humbly with God models for my children a reality that can produce happiness and not feelings of failure when they become adults. It's important that children know parents are humans who live on a budget, drop the ball sometimes, and always love them even when asking them to help with the yard work.

As we allow our children to see our human side, we also need them to see us seek God's guidance for our solutions as we address the challenges of life. This is the reason "walk humbly" is only part of the statement. We can't afford to miss the other part: "with your God." As life becomes challenging, we need to start by prayerfully looking at what God is doing in this circumstance. When my son was young, he discovered a sport he genuinely loved. It was fun to watch him play because he was very skilled and creative when doing so. Quickly he moved into the competitive leagues. It wasn't long into those leagues before a coach who originally thought he was fantastic came to the decision to cut him from his team. At that time, God sent an incredible young man into my son's life. He worked with my son on his running and agility. But more importantly, he taught my son to pray daily, "Thank you, God, for what you are doing in my life and for what you will do." This has carried my son through so many challenging and disappointing times. The prayer imparts the understanding that God is at work and that we can trust God as we move through the circumstance that seems to be so difficult. Also, it speaks of a willingness to trust God's time line and God's direction. My son continued to train and work hard, regardless of the circumstance. God worked on all the rest. Now, many years later, my son is learning that the time spent in agility and running work was incredibly beneficial for his development in his sport. God led him, my son trusted him, and we are still so thankful for all God has done, is doing, and will do in my son's life. This is just one of so many examples I can identify in the history of my life and my children's lives that clearly demonstrates that God is at work in our lives, even when it seems challenging. Walking with God means accepting that God is our authority and that we need to surrender to God's leading and God's timing. This can be complicated if we do not keep walking humbly in tandem with surrendering to God.

One of the best things we parents can do for our children is to pray with them daily prayers of thanksgiving. Thank God for what God is doing and what God will do. And discuss with your children how you can see God's hand at work in your past and present. Also take time to discuss with your children the process of prayer and study that will help them follow God and live out his purpose for their lives. God has a purpose we each are created to fulfill. If we are willing to submit to God's time line and leading, we will have the joy of discovering that purpose. If we are humbly walking with God, we will see things from God's perspective and not our own. This will make everything look different than it does from the world's perspective. Things we thought mattered greatly won't seem to matter any longer. Some of the circumstances that seem so discouraging will not retain importance when seen from

God's perspective. We need to be honest with ourselves and realize that our ideas and opinion of what is best and when it should happen is not the ideas and opinions we need. We should ask ourselves what God's opinion of how we perceive things is. What is God's opinion of what is best, and when it should happen? Often we don't have a clear answer to those questions. So we must respond with hope and faith, trusting God.

If we try to assert our own time lines, our own directions, or our own importance on circumstances, are we really walking with God? If I am striving to be in God's will, he will lead me to be the best possible parent for my kids. Honestly, isn't that what that deep parental love needs to bring out in us, a desire to walk humbly with our God and become the best parent possible for our children?

The Race Marked Out for You

Therefore, since we are surrounded by such a great cloud of witnesses, let us throw off everything that hinders and the sin that so easily entangles, and let us run with perseverance the race marked out for us.

—Hebrews 12:1 (NIV)

Don't blink—this will go by so fast. You hear this in song lyrics, you read it, and people older than you say it to you at the most inopportune moments: "Don't blink!" These days will go by so fast, and someday you will miss this, so don't blink. At the risk of sounding cliché, I'm here to tell you that those who say this are right. I can't believe how fast the time went from rocking my baby daughter to sleep to celebrating her twenty-first birthday and preparing to watch her graduate from college. In that flurry of calendar years flying by, I have so many memories of laughter, adventures, craft projects, wonderful conversations, and exciting times. I also remember feeling tired, defeated, and invisible, and fearing that I would always feel like that. At times it seemed that my life would forever be engulfed in small colorful plastic toys, laundry, and endless lunch packing. Then I blinked. My children grew so quickly that I genuinely do miss some of those times. My home is no longer cluttered with bright colored plastic toys, and I usually only need to do laundry once or twice a week. I miss the little hands reaching out to hold mine as we walk into the grocery store. Sometimes I even miss those little colorful plastic toys. I really miss those little voices laughing and the energetic approach to everything. To tell the truth, I miss coloring.

I remember when I was widowed. I looked down the eighteen-year-long road to my son's high school graduation and became completely overwhelmed with fear. How could I be all my children would need? Who would teach them what I could not? How would I endure this overwhelming loneliness for what appeared as a lifetime to me? Then I blinked! I blinked so quickly that eighteen-year-long road has raced under my feet, and the beautiful scenery that is the backdrop for countless memories has flown by far too fast.

> I will make you into a great nation and I will bless you;
> I will make your name great and you will be a blessing.
> (Genesis 12:2 NIV)

God made a promise to Abram, which represented a huge change for Abram's life. After this, Abram packed up all he had and moved his family to a new land. Later, God changed his name. Abraham heard the promise of a future from God, and then twenty-five years passed. He moved to foreign places. During those twenty-five years, God developed Abram's character into the character of Abraham. When we read about Abraham, we see the end result in the nation of Israel. But Abraham did not get to see it from the perspective we do when we read the scriptures. We can see the whole picture of what God was doing. We get to see beyond the twenty-five years of struggle and waiting and understand the work of God to transform Abram to Abraham. We also get to see the times when the twenty-five-year span of waiting took a toll on Abram and Sarai. But God could see the eternal perspective and was not worn out by the twenty-five-year wait.

God also sees our lives from his eternal perspective. Just like Abram and Sarai, we get discouraged or feel frustrated with the slow passing of time. If I am to be completely honest, I must say that there have been phases when the slow passing of time has taken a toll. I look in a mirror now and see a woman who gets invitations to AARP in the mail, not the young mother I was when I was widowed. There was a time when I would say I was a widow and people would say, "Oh my, you are so young to be widowed." Now, if I tell people I am widowed, they look at me and see a woman old enough to be a widow. While at times it feels like I have only blinked, I also feel the passing of time and wonder how there can be anything after this phase in my life. I think this often because I have placed an inaccurate expectation on what I think God should have done or should be doing. Like all of us, I can't see things from God's perspective of an eternal time line. I can't see the entire road, so I begin to think I am on an endless treadmill of disappointment, fatigue, frustration, and laundry. I need to remember that God is working from an eternal time line that is not subject to my impatience or frustration.

Abram became Abraham, and his descendants became so numerous that the Egyptians enslaved them and eventually feared their population growth. Moses, one of Abraham's descendants, was called to deliver the Israelites from slavery. He reluctantly set out with no knowledge of what was in front of him. His reluctance came out of his concern that he was not a skilled public speaker. Can you imagine how much he would have argued with God about going to face Pharaoh if he had known all that was actually ahead of him—plagues, deaths, walking through a sea, following a moving pillar through a desert? He thought public speaking was the most daunting part of what God was calling him to accomplish. He did not have a complete picture of what God was doing—and neither do we when we look at our own lives.

We are called to lead our children into the promised land of the life God has for them. We may have specific fears, but if we look back along all that we have come through, we will most likely see that the biggest challenge was not the one we feared. This is why we need to recognize that our ideas of what God should be doing and what we want from God are coming from a limited perspective. We need to accept that God is acting, and we must trust that. We must resist the urge to predict what God is going to do or to tell God what should be done. Rather, we need to take the steps that are directly in front of us, following God's leading. Like Abram, we need to make the move without asking exactly how many years until this promise will produce visible results. Count on God for the leading and the provisions of today. Like the manna in the desert, we can't store up tomorrow's bread. Enjoy today's bread, and trust in faith that the manna for tomorrow will be there.

Whether we signed up for this or not, we have a race marked out for us. God knows what is in that race. God knows how long the race is, what types of obstacles we will face, and how many obstacles we will face. God is running with us, and God has already gone in front of us to make the way ahead visible for us. We don't really want to know all the obstacles ahead; we just need strength and courage to run the race today. The length of the race only becomes overwhelming when we look beyond the stretch we can see today.

I once received some fantastic advice when I was still in college. I was told, "Expect nothing, and then you won't be disappointed." That sounds a bit cynical, but it has application here. I know I have the hardest, most frustrating days when I am tired and lonely. But what makes the frustration build faster than anything else is the voice in my head telling me that I will be more tired tomorrow and lonely forever. I am planning obstacles that are not in the stretch of the race I am running today. If I expect nothing, then I am not expecting fatigue tomorrow. Let the rested state or fatigue of tomorrow be revealed tomorrow. I add unnecessary stress to my load today by concerning myself with what tomorrow holds.

I also add unneeded anxiety when I worry about the length of this race I am running for my children. There is a great scene in the movie *Facing the Giants* where a football coach blindfolds a player and asks him to do a bear-crawl with another player on his back. Before they begin, he asks the player how far he thinks he can go. That number of yards becomes the goal, and then the blindfold is put on the player. He begins moving, and the coach is encouraging him. But the coach does not tell the boy how far he has really gone. Instead, he just keeps encouraging him. Soon the whole team is encouraging him. In the end, the player travels the length of the field, more than three times the distance he claimed as the goal. We all have that ability inside of us. God is encouraging us, and we are surrounded by so many people who are supporting us and cheering us on. We need to put on a blindfold to block our view of the actual distance and then just take one step at a time. Sometimes it does feel like we parents are actually crawling with our children on our backs. And metaphorically we are. We must remember that God will provide all we need to go the full length of the race set out before us.

You do not need to be concerned with the distance of the race. God will take all the time needed to grow your character and transform you just as he did Abram and Sarai. God will provide for you and equip you to meet the demands of his call for your life. If his calling seems like a task greater than you can manage, know that God will work in you to prepare you to handle his assignment. God will present the people to help you when you need them. God will give you understanding and knowledge as you need it.

It is our job as parents to see the burning bushes in our lives and respond with faith. It is important that we allow our children to witness us stopping and listening when we see a burning bush. They need to witness us responding and going in the directions God calls. By our modeling of this, they will learn to do the same in their lives.

God calls us to walk a different path from that of anyone else. We each get our own burning bushes and a specific call from them. Each one of us has a unique and different path. Don't take your eyes off God and his calling and directions in order to focus on others. I will tell you that each time I see someone my age find a person with whom to share his or her life, it hurts. It makes me question why I am not in that person's situation. It intensifies my loneliness and elevates my frustrations. All I really need to do to avoid this is to be aware of and purposeful about where I am focusing. When I strive to focus my energy on the race God has set out for me, I don't struggle with those frustrations and pains. When I put energy into *my* race, everything works better.

To run our own race well, we need to focus our energy on the things that matter most, and that will enhance our ability to throw off everything that hinders and entangles us. We need to keep a balanced life as we live out the priorities we are trying to teach our children. We need to maintain our spiritual health through scripture study, worship, prayer, and quiet times. We need to maintain our physical health through attention to regular exercise, healthy eating habits, reasonable sleep patterns, and attempts to reduce the amount of stress we accept in our lives. We need to nurture and protect our family relationships by taking time to be present with each other and generating places and times to communicate and have "real talk" time with each other. We need to maintain our professional work commitments in a balanced way that upholds our standard of excellence for our work but does not compromise the family relationships that are a higher priority. Finally, we need to establish ways to maintain our home that will keep the household running smoothly without tipping the scale of balanced use of time. That should be enough to fill our focus. We don't need to be looking at other people and the perceived "better situation" we think they have. I once heard a sweet southern woman say this: "I just stay in my lane." That is wise and wonderful! I think my lane has plenty for me to focus on and tend to. I have no need to look into another lane while I am driving in my own. I am going to strive to stay in my lane.

Keeping all that is genuinely important or necessary in balance is demanding. Sometimes I have to overlap tasks to get all the pieces of this balancing act to stay together. I have learned that functioning as a family unit, supporting each other in our activities, can also provide great "real talk" time in the car as we drive from one place to another. To prevent the use of headphones, I listen to the music my children would choose. (Yes, that is a sacrifice on my part!) My children also get to work on family support and teamwork as we all pitch in around the house to keep it clean and maintained. I have learned to slip in my exercise for the day while a child is practicing a sport or getting math tutoring. I taught driving skills to one child while the other was in reading tutoring.

This balancing act is the race set before me. Keeping it all free of that which would hinder or entangle me is plenty work. I will just stay in my lane and focus my eyes on the race God has set out for me to run.

We need to keep in mind that within scripture, we read, "The race is marked out for us." That means there are markings and directions as we go. We need to remember daily that God is with us, guiding us, and providing others to help us when we need it. We are not running blindly or without guidance. The race is marked out. We need to look at the markers and heed the directions we are given. We need to remain aware and thankful for all that God is doing. This will help us keep our focus on all that is in our own race. Also, it will help us model a life skill that is the most important skill we can teach our children: to identify the presence of God, see the role models and the people God places in our lives, and hear the promptings of the Holy Spirit.

It is part of human nature to look at the lives of others and feel envious. But keep in mind, it is not just a sweet southern woman with wisdom saying, "I just stay in my lane"; scripture offers this as well:

> Peter turned and saw the disciple whom Jesus loved
> following them. This was the one who had leaned against
> Jesus at the meal and asked him. "Lord, who is going to
> betray you?" When Peter saw this disciple, he said to
> Jesus, "Lord, what about him?" Jesus replied, "If I want
> him to remain until I come, what difference does that
> make to you? You must follow me." (John 21:20–21 CEB)

Don't take your eyes off God and his calling and direction to focus on other servants. Be aware of your focus, and do as the Hebrews scripture states—throw off all that hinders. In the scripture from John 21, Peter had just received from Jesus the opportunity to declare his love for Jesus and his willingness to follow Jesus. When Jesus says to Peter, "Follow me," Peter instantly looks at another disciple. Peter had just received from Jesus words regarding his own future, and then he looked at the situation of another disciple. I know I am so much like Peter, looking at the circumstances of others and comparing. I look at the ministry that God has given to others and compare my ministry. But God has called me to my own unique ministry. I need to keep my focus on my ministry. I look at the relationships and friendships that others enjoy and compare mine with theirs. But God has called me to a set of fantastic relationships and friendships in my own life. I need to keep my focus on those. I look at the blessings in the lives of those around me and compare them to my own. But God has blessed me with what I need to guide and lead my children to the promised land of the life he has for them. I need to keep my focus on the blessings I have and be thankful for the provisions God has placed in our lives to accomplish what he wills for my children and for me. Just like Peter, we must not compare. Jesus assigned Peter to walk a different path than John. And just like Peter, we need to hear Jesus saying, "You must follow me."

> Turning around Jesus saw them following and asked
> "What do you want?" They said, "Rabbi (which means
> "Teacher"), where are you staying?" "Come," he replied
> "and you will see." So they went and saw where he was

staying, and they spent that day with him. (John 1:38–39 NIV)

Here we get an account of two men who would become disciples, one of them Andrew, whom later Jesus names Peter. There is some history here that we must address. Andrew had listened to John the Baptist preach about the coming Messiah. Now he was meeting Jesus. He must have had so many questions about his ministry and what the future would hold. He didn't get a sit-down conversation. Rather he received a directive: "Come." Andrew followed. Andrew would experience on a day-by-day basis the ministry of Jesus and what the future held. I often feel like this is a great lesson for us to learn. Jesus is saying to us, "Come. The race is marked out; the way is going to be made clear. Focus on me and come." Our questions will be answered as we run with perseverance the race marked out for us.

> Moments will come when you stand at a crossroads with your Lord. You will have a hundred questions for Him. Rather than answering the questions one by one, Jesus may say, "Put on your shoes, step out on the road, and follow me." As you walk daily with Him, Jesus will answer your questions, and you will discover far more than you even knew to ask.[1]

The race in front of us entails raising our children to love God and live lives that are faith directed and faith driven. This race will have obstacles and cover an unknown distance. We will face enough obstacles in the race without adding to them by letting our focus wander away from following the directive "Come." We must stay focused and avoid looking too far ahead, comparing our lives to the lives of others, or questioning what God is accomplishing as he is fulfilling his purpose in our lives and in the lives of our children. Listen to his voice as he coaches you and encourages you to finish this race!

---

[1] H. Blackaby and R. Blackaby, *Experiencing God Day by Day* (Nashville: B&H Books, 2006), 25.

Prepare Your Children for Battle

But since we belong to the day, let us be self-controlled, putting on faith and love as a breastplate, and the hope of salvation as a helmet.

—1 Thessalonians 5:8 (NIV)

My daughter was a toddler when we got her a big-girl bed. We set it up in her room with great care. I was so worried that she would fall out of bed and hurt herself that night. I lost sleep as I worried about her while she slept. She slept soundly. She did not worry about falling out of bed. I couldn't shake my fear of her falling out of bed and getting hurt. Finally morning came, and I went into her room to check on her. There she was sound asleep, resting very comfortably on the floor beside her bed. She was sleeping so soundly that when she fell out of bed, she just kept right on sleeping without interruption or pain.

Isn't this how so many parenting stories often read? We worry about potential injury or damage for our children, and most often, they are not nearly as hurt as we fear. Also true, though, is that they are going to grow up, let go of our hands, run off, stumble and fall, and get hurt. If they don't stumble on their own, at some point they will encounter someone who will trip them. As much as we want the entire world to be child-safe, it isn't. As much as we want every friend to be a good friend for our children, they aren't. We don't want life to knock our kids down. But more importantly, we don't want our kids to lack the ability to get up after they are knocked down. We all have been knocked down, and as I wrote earlier, we know participation trophies are doing more harm than good, so it stands to reason that a childhood without any knockdown moments is going to cause our children to lack the strength to pick themselves up. We need to prepare them for the real life, which is, living in this fallen world. We may feel this is a potentially impossible task, but we are led by One who gives us the strength to say that we can do all things through Christ (paraphrase of Philippians 4:13).

We can start by working to give our children the tools Christ carried with him into the wilderness. Right after Jesus was baptized by John the Baptist, he went into the desert and was tempted. We find an account of this in Matthew chapter 4, Mark chapter 1, and Luke chapter 4. Jesus battles the temptations in the desert with his knowledge of scripture, an unshakable identity as the Son of God, and a clear understanding of his purpose as the Messiah. We need to arm our children with a strong knowledge of scripture, an unshakable identity as children of God, and the ability to discern and have an understanding of their God-directed purpose.

We can arm our children with a strong knowledge of scripture in many ways. We need to recognize that children have different learning styles. I contend that we should use as many different ways to imprint God's Word on their hearts and in their minds as we can. Do not use only one approach.

> Hear, O Israel: The Lord our God, the Lord is one. Love the Lord your God with all your heart and with all your soul and with all your strength. These commandments that I give you today are to be upon your hearts. Impress them on your children. Talk about them when you sit at home and when you walk along the road, when you lie down and when you get up. Tie them as symbols on your hands and bind them on your doorframes of your houses and on your gates. (Deuteronomy 6:4–9 NIV)

Teach the scriptures diligently to your children, and discuss them in your home regularly. This does not imply there should be study sessions with debate and quizzes. I am proposing that you facilitate the diligent study of scripture in many ways. Regular attendance in Sunday school classes and small group studies are a great start. Since our children learn in different ways, use a variety of approaches at home. There are many video options for teaching scriptures to children at every age level. There are also music presentations that can teach scripture to your children. While my children were young, we listened to children's music that taught scripture to kids through songs in the car. Before they could read, they could sing the names of the books of the Bible in order. Your local Christian bookstore or an online Christian bookstore is a fantastic resource for discovering what is available for your children and appropriate for their age. Let scripture appear in your home. Ask your children to make art for your refrigerator that has scripture in it. There are coloring books and art resources to help with this. Make ornaments for the Christmas tree that depict a variety of scripture stories. When it is time for a bedtime story, read your children a story from the Bible. As your children grow, teach them the ways scripture can answer our life dilemmas. If you are not confident in guiding your children in this, avail yourself of resources at a Christian bookstore or online. Learn together with your children as questions are answered through study. This shows them how to search for answers and study by modeling. If your older children are attracted to art, there are scripture-based coloring books for adults that they might enjoy. Most important in all of this is the discussion aspect. As your responses to life and decisions are influenced by your understandings from scripture, share those thoughts in conversation with your children. Let them learn through you how the scriptures are the living Word of God.

If faith is not based in scripture, then one must ask, "What exactly do you believe?" It is critical to faith development that a knowledge and love of the scriptures is encouraged and practiced. When faith-driven people are questioned, they should have a clear understanding of what they believe and the foundation for that belief. This also empowers us to walk our beliefs on a daily basis.

Knowledge of scripture is also strength and power for living in our circumstances. Jesus withstood the temptations in the desert because his knowledge of scripture gave him strength and kept his focus on his purpose. If you immerse yourself daily in scripture, then when the crisis comes, you will not be caught off guard or with a faith that will not run. It is like maintaining a car—keep it in tune, and it runs for years and years. Scripture is the substance and the maintenance of your faith. You would not give your child a car to drive that had never been tuned up or maintained. Be diligent to set your children on the road of life with a finely tuned vehicle of faith. Scriptural knowledge will give your children strength as well as guidance. Scripture spells out the pitfalls of life to avoid, such as greed, gluttony, pride, envy, lust, and wrath. Scripture gives us a clear picture of how to respond to the injured, those who are judged by society, and those who seek grace and forgiveness. Preparing our children for the battle of life ahead, giving them a strong knowledge of scriptures by taking every opportunity to instruct them in a variety of approaches, is not something we want to do sparingly.

> Remember this: "Whoever sows sparingly will also reap sparingly, and whoever sows generously will also reap generously." (2 Corinthians 9:6 NIV)

It is our task to teach our children as if the knowledge is seed and we are sowing generously. We may attempt to instruct them in a way that they don't receive well. But if we are taking multiple approaches, sowing generously, then the harvest will come. We can't allow them to take a shallow approach to their relationship with God. We need to teach them to cultivate their relationship with God through study, spiritual discipline, and prayer. We teach through instruction, through life lessons, and through modeling. What they see is what they will emulate.

In addition to a strong knowledge of scripture, we need to arm our children with an unshakable identity as children of God. Our children need to know without question that they are deeply loved and greatly valued by God. Our children can use the scriptural knowledge they have to understand God's desire for a relationship with them. We need to complement that knowledge with experiences of love and grace that we extend to them. This will give them the experience reference of a loving, grace-giving parent. As parents we should strive to model and live out grace and unconditional love so that our children come to see the grace and love of God as a reality. Our children will come to understand the relationship God wants them to seek in a variety of ways, and one of those ways is as we model grace and unconditional love. They can read through scripture the accounts of God's efforts to establish a relationship with his creation. They can experience God's love and the relationship one can have with God through worship and daily living experiences.

> But we have this treasure in jars of clay to show that
> this all-surpassing power is from God and not from us.
> (2 Corinthians 4:7 NIV)

This is a fantastic demonstration of scripture used to emphasize God's love for us. Clay jars were commonly used for containers at the time this scripture was written. The jars would become chipped and broken and worn over time, and no one gave any thought to that. The thought was given to the contents of the jar. What was within the jar was of importance. That was what had value, and that is what was interesting to those who owned the jars. Paul is telling us that we are like those jars. What is important to God is what he has placed within us— not the condition, attractiveness, or beauty of the jar. The container is not of concern to God; the contents are! God has placed immeasurable value within us by the power of the Holy Spirit. This is what we should value, and this is what makes us a treasure to God. We need to teach our children how infinitely valuable they are to God because of what God has placed within them. Every opportunity we have to share that, point to that virtue, and nurture that understanding should be maximized. We need to take every opportunity to emphasize and teach to our children how deeply they are loved and valued by God! They need to know deeply that God loves them and treasures them.

An aspect of grace and unconditional love that is often overlooked is accountability and boundaries. It is easy to confuse a lack of boundaries as a means of unconditional love, but such is not the case. Holding them accountable and enforcing boundaries is the best way to love our children. It takes energy to hold our children accountable, and it takes unconditional love to expect the best from them and hold them within boundaries to guide them to be the best they can be. It is easy to allow ourselves to confuse unconditional love and grace with a lack of discipline and accountability. We need to make a conscious effort to make sure our children know the grace we extend is not an opportunity to make decisions that lead them outside the acceptable boundaries without consequences. The grace we extend them shows we love them regardless of the times they don't stay within the boundaries, and more, that we love them enough to enforce the boundaries. Accountability partnered with grace and unconditional love is defined by consistent boundaries that are supported by predictable consequences.

Accountability is a part of any relationship. As our children learn accountability, they gain strength in their relationship with God. As they hold themselves accountable for their own daily walk with God, they will solidify their identity as children of God. Holding children accountable is a great way to enable them to gain the skills to hold themselves accountable. I believe a lack of accountability is one of the seeds of failures in adult life—educational failures, relationship failures, professional failures, personal failures, and financial failures. If children are held accountable, they will learn that skill, hopefully apply it to themselves, and allow it to determine how they address issues in adulthood. The most important aspect of accountability is how it will strengthen your child's identity as a child of God. Ultimately we need to do all we can to empower our children to seek God as their Father and to turn to God as the ultimate parent rather than look toward an earthly parent who will inevitably fail them at some point.

Where I grew up, we had lots of fruit trees in our backyard. When the trees were first planted in our backyard, I was ready for the fresh fruit that day! Sadly, I learned at a young age that the fruit doesn't grow on the tree right away. The tree must first grow a strong root system so the growth of the tree can be nourished. Then the tree must grow stronger through the branches and the trunk. Only when the roots are firmly established and the trunk and branches are strong enough to support the weight of the growing fruit will the tree begin to produce. One of the challenges of parenting and attempting to raise a child who will bear an abundance of the fruits of the Holy Spirit is that we don't always get to be there for the harvest. Often as parents, we are only there to nurture the root system as it gets established. The young adult child is the one who works to grow the trunk and branches stronger. Then, when we no longer are fixing them a lunch for school, the fruit comes. We may not be present to see it, but we get to experience the joy of knowing about it.

Our job is to nurture the roots and establish the practices and habits that will strengthen the branches and the trunk. While we wish we could be there to enjoy the sweet fruit, we need to be prepared for the possibility that we most likely will not be present daily when the sweet fruit appears. Regardless, we must do all we can to provide for our children a root system that connects them to God as their Father. As our children grow, we need to guide them with boundaries and accountability so the trunk and branches gain strength.

As we prepare our children for the battle of life, we must include the significant tool of a clear purpose. We must recognize that our children are growing up in a time that generates a struggle in this area. When a child has a clear sense of purpose and direction, it is far more difficult for the pressures of life to sway that child off track. Finding what that purpose is, and keeping it in sight over a long span of time, is a challenge for anyone. Unfortunately, our children are led by current culture to begin this challenge already limited. Social media and a culture of instant results and instant gratification will stunt the growth of a strong work ethic and the ability to focus on long-range goals.

We need to teach our children to work for the long-range goals. My dad would say, "If it's worth having, it's worth working for." Social media and instant digital results have taught young people to expect instant gratification. That is psychologically unfulfilling. We must teach them that things that genuinely matter take time and hard work—and we must help them gain the skills to put in the work and endure the struggle to get the results that are psychologically and emotionally fulfilling.

The Andy Griffith Show from the 1960s aired an episode in which Andy, the dad, tries to express to Opie, the young son, that sometimes you do things (like clean the garage) for "the good feeling" you get when you accomplish it. Of course, the young boy struggles to accept that he should "work for the good feeling," but he follows his father's advice and does clean the garage. For our children, very little requires them to work hard and go for the good feeling of achieving something over a long period of time. Don't hesitate to have your children do the hard work that will generate that good feeling. They may be like Opie and doubt that the good feeling is worth the work. The benefit of allowing them to experience that rewarding feeling is immeasurably valuable.

Recently while I was doing a large project around our home, my son and his friends agreed to help. The project required several days of genuinely hard physical work. The first day of work, there were six teenage boys working in the yard. On the second day there were three teenage boys working. When the fourth and final day arrived, there were only two boys left, and one was my son. The hard work without instant results was more than most of the boys could endure. Long-term work for genuine results has become a rare experience for too many of our children. We parents need to purposefully build this into their experiences, if not around our own homes, then around the homes of others. There are simple ways to create these opportunities to help with large tasks in your own home or to extend help to neighbors. Other opportunities can be found in donating time to participate in a Habitat for Humanity build (the minimum age requirement must be met) or participate in work with a local relief agency. We need to realize we giving our children not only the opportunity to learn how to work for a long-range goal but also an opportunity to build confidence through hard work.

When my son was about twelve he wanted an in-ground basketball hoop. This would require digging a large hole, mixing cement, and constructing all the pieces to put up his basketball hoop. He worked for several days on this project. The best part of the project for me was watching my son's confidence go up as the hoop went up. As we parents are working to instill the ability to work for a long-term goal, we need to recognize that a child needs confidence to set a long-term goal and accept a call from God. Hard work does instill confidence. We all want to have a sense of purpose. The ability to discern a long-term goal requires the confidence and emotional endurance to work toward the long-term goal. Both of these are crucial to discerning one's purpose.

How to reach long-term goals is not just taught through experiences of long hard tasks in the yard or on a Habitat for Humanity build site. Our children also need to learn to endure struggles through other situations that can generate a need for emotional endurance, like learning a difficult subject in school or developing a challenging skill set. When my daughter became interested in martial arts, I gathered information from the various schools in our area. Some of the schools assured me that she would learn to defend herself and gain confidence. Other schools assured me that in only a matter of weeks, she would advance through various belt colors and experience lots of success. I placed her in the school that assured me she would be able to defend herself. I worked with her to understand that working for the long span of time needed to achieve the next color of belt was a good thing. Not only did she eventually gain an adult black belt, but also she learned to work for long periods of time to achieve a meaningful goal.

Because of the importance, we need to do more than expose our children to opportunities to experience the realization of a long-term goal. We should teach our children why they are challenged by a need for instant gratification. They need to be armed with the knowledge of how and why our culture is training them to lack this skill. Teach your children about the dopamine that is released in the human brain, giving a momentary false sense of acceptance and satisfaction. As our children reach adolescence, it is important that they understand how they are created. Dopamine is a chemical released in the brain. It is released under several circumstances, but among these are when a person gambles, drinks, or smokes, or when the cell phone alert interrupts them. The need in adolescence for peer approval is part of a normal psychological development stage. The issue is when dopamine generates the false sense of approval. Then the seeds of addiction to the activity that generated the dopamine response are planted. Our children need to understand this danger. Dopamine is what generates addiction to all those activities previously listed, including social media. Dopamine also generates an addiction to instant results and instant responses because of the social media format. The end result is that our children become addicted to instant gratification. What they do not realize is that instant gratification is psychologically unfulfilling. We must teach them that the things that genuinely matter take time and hard work—and help them gain the skills to put in the work and endure the struggle to get the results that are psychologically and emotionally fulfilling.

We are in danger of raising kids who do not have the skills to work for a long-term objective. Scripture and faith teaches our children to want to make an impact for the kingdom, so we also need to teach them how to work long term to make that impact and encourage them to realize how often we will not actually see the full impact of our work until much later, if at all. We need to guide and teach our children in the skill of goal setting and goal orientation. There were so many times my children faced the typical teen pressures, and because they had long-range goals, the pressures could be neutralized by simply reminding them they had goals and too much to lose. By helping them set long-term goals, I did not have to fight against teen pressures in the way many parents often experience. My task became finding ways to keep the long-range goals at the forefront of my children's thinking.

Guiding children to discern purpose in their lives is a tremendously important part of our job as parents. Without a sense of purpose, there is no need to set goals. We need to engage them in conversations and also teach them to listen to the promptings of the Holy Spirit. We also need to help them understand the variety of purposes we each have. As disciples we all have the same overriding purpose to be witnesses and living testaments to the Gospel. As uniquely created individuals, we have a distinct purpose driven by the gifts that God has blessed each of us with. Each of us is created with talents and gifts enabling us to glorify God and bring glory to the kingdom in specific ways. These talents are to be invested to grow the awareness of the goodness of God. As our children become aware of the talents that are a part of who they are, they can learn how those talents indicate and lead them to their purpose. They can also learn to listen to the promptings of the Holy Spirit on a heartfelt level and allow those heartfelt desires to lead them to understand their unique purpose.

To restate, we all share the overriding purpose to be a witness and living testament to the Gospel. It is important we begin when they are very young helping our children understand that the way they live and behave may be the only Gospel message some people ever see. I have used several wonderful analogies of this with my children. I have told them they may be the only sermon a person ever hears or the only gospel a person ever reads. The one they seemed to respond to best was the question, if Christianity were illegal, would there be enough evidence in your life to convict you? As parents we need to purposefully seek opportunities to remind our children of the powerful witness they have in their daily lives. We also need to be aware of our own witness in how we are living and how we are treating those around us, because our children are watching us. On one particular occasion when I had become a bit more vocal and excited at a football game than I should have, I had to confess to my children that I was in the wrong. In doing that, I made certain to use the moment as a teaching moment, and instead of just saying "I blew that," I said, "I compromised my witness today, and I am sorry." They need to know their parents are human, but we parents also need to be aware that we are constantly a witness to the goodness of God.

As your children seek to use the God-given talents and passions they have and discover a personal purpose, it is important you teach them one significant lesson I learned from a peer while I was in college. I was racing bicycles and was blessed to have a group of training partners who were excellent athletes and very experienced racers. One day while we were out training, the best of the group started a conversation with me as we rode. He asked me why I liked to win races. I told him that I liked to win to bring glory to God. He responded, "God doesn't need your trophies." He then rode on ahead. He eventually rode beside me again, and we repeated the exchange. After doing this a few times, I finally realized my answer was not satisfactory, so I replied with, "Why do you think I like to win?" His reply changed my thinking for the rest of my life. He said, "You like to win for yourself. It makes you happy. Don't feel bad about that. God wants you to feel joy and happiness. But if you want to bring glory to God, pay attention to how you win. It is *how* you do what you do that will bring glory to God." I never forgot that moment when I realized *how* I do things, the way I go about all I do, will bring glory to God. I work very hard to remind my children of this as often as I can.

Once your children believe they have found a purpose, the goal setting can begin. If your children are not able to discover a passion or a lifelong purpose, help them set long-range goals that will help them remain focused and driven until the time when they have a stronger sense of individual purpose. I have two children, and they are as different as any two can be in this area. One had a struggle to find a sense of lifelong purpose, whereas the other felt certain of that purpose when only eight or nine years old. Either way, they both set long-range goals that were important and presented them with too much to lose when the peer pressure started to mount.

While the one was driven to achieve a long-range purpose from a very early age, and all of the long-range goals seemed to direct the path for accomplishing that goal, the other child set long-range goals to lead to opportunities for discovering that purpose later. Working toward achieving a spot on a varsity team or a high-level honor in a specific endeavor keeps focus and teaches hard work toward a delayed-gratification payoff. Additionally, setting goals of academic achievement so the options after high school would not be limited became important. Whichever way your child is wired, work within that design to accomplish this teaching.

Discuss with your children regularly that God has a plan for them. It does not matter if they have a clear sense of the specifics of God's plan. Teach them to see the blessings that surround them daily and how those can help identify an individual purpose. For example, when my son started middle school he was interested in playing football. It was not a simple choice. He had already invested a lot of energy in a sport he genuinely felt passionate about—soccer. His soccer coaches did not want him to play football. He wanted to fit in with his peers at school and play football, but he did not want to risk injury. He decided he would learn how to be a placekicker. We talked about it, and this seemed to be a great solution. Neither of us knew placekicking is completely different from kicking a soccer ball.

As football started, he was making very little progress as a kicker. The coaches were patient, but he was not feeling good about how he was performing. Every Sunday on our way to church we would pass by a practice field and see a coach teaching boys how to kick. After seeing this a few times and talking about it, I felt convicted to stop and ask the coach for information. It turned out the coach was a former NFL kicker. He has now been coaching my son for a few years and has generated significant progress. I believe God led us to this coach. I am not going to say that I believe placekicking is my son's purpose. What I can say is that as my son has gained ground as a kicker, he has often talked about the coach, his profession as a coach, and how he could see himself coaching kids when he is an adult. Time will tell, but my son's purpose may very well be in the area of touching children's lives through coaching. I purposefully tell my children when I believe God has led one of us in a specific direction. I work to point out as many situations like this as I can. God has placed many people in my children's lives who point them in the direction of the purpose God has designed them to accomplish.

What is important is that your children realize, and hear from you often, that God designed them with a unique set of traits and talents for a specific purpose. Sometimes that purpose seems larger than life and is something your children can use to set lifelong goals. Other times there are only small hints. These are moments in time where your child's unique gifts are revealed and a nudge in the direction of a future shows.

My daughter had run to the grocery store for just a few items, and it seemed to take an extremely long time for her to come back home. When she arrived, she told me that what had caused the delay was an encounter in the store. She passed a father and daughter in the area where women's shaving supplies are shelved. As she walked past, she overheard the discussion and clear confusion about the products and options. Having grown up with only one living parent, she felt compassion for the teen girl who was looking overwhelmed and anxious. Moved to action, my daughter stopped and offered help and advice. She took time to explain the products she recommended and even took time to talk the younger girl through the process of shaving her legs. When she finished and was walking away, she heard the dad tell the girl how thankful he was for the help. My daughter said the young girl had looked relieved and happy as she was finishing giving them advice and information. My daughter saw anxiety in a young girl, and she was moved to help. It seems like a small moment, but for a young woman who was trying to determine if psychology was the correct major in college, it was an important moment for my daughter. She felt affirmed in the decision she was making with regard to her college major. This is how God can nudge, direct, and affirm us as we seek to realize our purpose.

You can share your own experiences with this and find examples, such as faith-driven success stories, that have made an impact on the world for the kingdom of God. It is also good to point out those with public acclaim who have fallen short. They can show the importance of attending to your faith and witness. It is also very important for your children to hear you reflect on your own journey. Every time your children hear about the ways God led and directed you or others to realize their individual purpose, it assures them that God can do the same for them. As our children grow, they will encounter phases where the path God is leading them along seems clear and where setting long-range goals seems simple. They will also encounter phases where the path God is leading them along seems mysterious and difficult to follow. During times like these, help your children to set and work toward shorter-range goals, creating steps toward a general longer-range goal. Goal setting is a skill many people don't naturally possess. We need to teach it to our children so they can stay focused on the purpose God has created them to live out. As they move into adulthood, the understanding that they are living the purpose God created for them to live is a powerful weapon to use when they deal with the battles of life accompanying adulthood.

As you strive to help your children recognize God's hand in their lives, build the habit of prayer. Consistent multiple daily prayer times are a vital part of communication with God. Communication is crucial to maintaining a relationship with God and hearing God's direction and leading in our lives. Build moments of prayer into the daily aspects of life: morning prayers, mealtime prayers, prayers before taking tests at school, prayers over special events, prayer at the end of every day. Lay the foundation of prayer as a natural part of daily living. The closeness generated by communication is not limited to human relationships. We can feel greater closeness with God when we maintain communication.

As my children grew up, we began with regular prayer throughout the day and always ended the day with a prayer of thanksgiving and the Lord's Prayer before bed. One time when I was away for work, I was sitting in the quiet hotel room and my phone rang. It was my son calling because he could not go to bed without our prayer time together at the end of the day. My heart was filled with joy that our praying together was this important to him already.

I am doing all I can to prepare my children for the battle of a life following God's purpose. Prayer is significant in that it opens the lines of communication for our children to talk to and hear from God. It also nurtures the relationship our children need with God. Making sure they communicate with God is telling them to "go ask your dad about that." As they learn to pray and build communication, they will also learn to hear Dad's response to all the questions they bring to him. This reinforces their identity as children of God. Nothing can be more important for your children than grounding them in the identity of "child of God." Pray with them often, and teach them to make prayer a regular part of every day.

As my children have grown, I wish I could say that the hardest thing they ever encountered was not falling out of bed. I can't say that, and neither can any other parent. Our children encounter struggles and battles that break our hearts. The good news is that we can give them the tools for battle and prepare them. We can arm them with the knowledge of scripture, a solid identity as a child of God, and a clear sense of purpose for their adult life. We can't fight the battle of life for them, but God will be with them every step of the way, one he has already prepared for them.

Our Children Will Do What We Do, Not What We Say

—————◇—————

I will take my post; I will position myself on the fortress.
I will keep watch to see what the Lord says to me and
how he will respond to my complaint.

—Habakkuk 2:1 (CEB)

The application of this verse to a parent's life is that we are the ones on the watchtower—we are the ones standing guard. We are the watchmen for ourselves and our families. We must take hold of the reality that we are the ones on the fortress wall for our children. It would be wonderful if that only meant we needed to be vigilant for what touches their lives and what our children touch. Unfortunately, it is not that simple. We must also be vigilant of the things they see us touch and what we allow to touch our lives.

I have had more moments than I can count where I am certain my voice sounded like the voice of the adults from the *Peanuts* cartoon shows. In case you've never seen those classic shows, every time an adult speaks, all the audience hears is an incomprehensible "Wha, wha, wha, wha." I would speak to my children, giving them instructions or asking them to do something, and no sooner would I finish speaking than they would prove they had not heard what I was saying. Of course, as soon as they got a driver's license, they proved they had been watching how I drive. This was not exactly a positive approach to driving. Unfortunately no matter what I told them and no matter what the drivers' education program told them, they did what they had seen me do.

I will never forget the time I came to the preschool to pick my daughter up and was greeted by her teacher, who did not look happy. Her greeting was "We need to have a talk." Evidently after spilling a canister of buttons, my daughter stood over them with her hands on her hips and said something much more adult than preschool. The mannerism and phrasing was exactly something her dad would exhibit and say when he was exasperated. She had watched him and learned precisely how to execute the phrase and in what context it should be used, all by simply observing.

Don't allow yourself to believe your children are not watching and learning. They will learn more from watching you than you will teach them while talking to them. If you want your children to study scripture, make sure they see you study. If you want your children to pray about things, allow them to pray with you or see you praying about the things on your heart. If you want your son to drive within the posted speed limit, let him see you drive the speed limit. If you want your children to have a strong work ethic, let them see you work hard at the things you do. If you want your daughter to value her education and her intellect, let her see you continue to strive for intellectual growth. What you value and pursue, they will value and pursue. This is not a fail-proof plan. I have seen children in my classes who did not fit this pattern. But for the most part, it is common for them to hear us parents speak with our actions far more clearly than they hear us speak with our words.

It is our task to model the behaviors and the practices that will serve our children well. We must be aware that we are the ones on watch for their lives, so what we say and do matters. We can't tell our children they should work hard to accomplish what is important to them over the long term and then allow them to see us taking shortcuts or putting in half efforts at the tasks in front of us. If we tell our children the approval they should seek needs to come from God and not earthly sources, and if they see us frantically trying to find dating relationships to fill the empty space left by our single status, we have destroyed the message we spoke. We need to recognize that as we live our lives on a day-to-day basis, we are teaching our children some of the most indelible lessons they will learn. We are on the watchtower for our children, and that makes it easy for them to see us. It is difficult and painful to take the hard look at ourselves this requires. I don't want to admit that my weaknesses and faults are plentiful. I also don't want to admit that those weaknesses and faults can be passed on to my children by my example. As painful as it is, I need to make sure that what I carry up the watchtower with me is what I want my children to see and to do. That will require a great deal of self-examination and self-discipline. This includes what is posted on our social media as well. If we want our children to be humble, then posting only the best photos of the greatest moments is counter to that lesson. If we want our children to value time with their friends that does not need to involve alcohol, then posting "girls' night out" pictures of having drinks at a bar for our children and their friends to see is not supportive of that message. This is a hard topic. I once heard this set of phrases: Watch your thoughts because they become your words; watch your words because they become actions; watch your actions because they become habits; watch your habits because they define your character; and watch your character because it sets your destiny. This is worth repeating: it is an extremely hard topic and one that needs examination. If our children will do what they see in us, then it is logical that what they see in us will determine their character and destiny. Not only is this an extremely hard topic, but also it is a convicting topic.

I often get this response from people on this difficult topic: "I am the adult. They need to understand it is different because they are children." My reply is simply this: "They are children, and you need to understand from their perspective, using the reasoning of a child. They are not going to understand why you get to have a different set of rules running counter to what you expect of them. Additionally, they are only living in your home with you for a limited amount of time. The time will come when you can climb down out of the watchtower because they will have their own families and it will be their time to be on the tower. Your watchtower time will pass very quickly, and you will not miss the habits you removed because the watchtower did not have room for them. You will be filled with joy over the family you are standing watch over and watching them mature. Their imitating your example of living will bring so much fulfillment and joy that you won't even remember the things you removed."

We are all aware there are habits and practices simply needing removal because of our place on the watchtower. Make sure you are carrying with you the important things the watchtower requires. You need to take a healthy prayer life with you. I speak of this often, but prayer is the vital communication link maintaining your relationship with God. This practice needs to be firmly established in your children. Realize that if they see you make decisions without prayer, if they never hear you say "I need to pray about that" and they never witness you asking others to pray for you, they likely will not establish this communication for themselves. As small children, we learn to talk and communicate by listening and observing and then imitating. So give your children something to observe and imitate as they seek to establish communication with God.

I have written about the prayer my son was taught to pray by a coach: "Thank you, God, for what you are doing in my life and what you will do." This powerful faith statement gained support when I prayed with him and also prayed that prayer. There were times when he was so discouraged that he wasn't sure he could pray that prayer, so I prayed for him: "Thank you, God, for what you are doing in his life and what you will do." It not only set an example for him but also affirmed my faith and confidence in what God was doing. It is good for our children to see and hear us pray so they will have that example to follow.

Another practice that must be visible to our children in the watchtower is the priority of our relationship with God. How we spend our time is a strong indication of our priorities. If our children never see us attend to our relationship with God, how will they know how to maintain a healthy faith relationship for themselves? They need to see us study, take quiet moments, attend worship, sing, and express the joy of a faith-filled life. If you look at your schedule and find there is no evidence of a relationship with God in your daily activities, then you need to make room in the watchtower for adding these moments. Don't worry if your study and quiet times are before your children wake up. They will become aware that you get up early to study and have quiet time. They will see the strength you gain from that time. They will see the Bible, books, and journal you are using, and they will know. My children were rarely awake during my personal study times while they were growing up, but they knew what I did each morning, and in this way the example was set. When they see this example as a part of daily living and woven into the fabric of the relationships and profession you maintain, they will learn how to establish their relationship with God as the first priority. This gives them a model of what it is to maintain earthly relationships while knowing these are second to a relationship with God. If we want our children to be able to resist peer pressure and crowd following, we need to model wanting God and God's will the very most!

While we are on the watchtower, we need to be purposeful in modeling faith responses to life's struggles and conflicts. We often want to respond to the hurts of life and the struggles of life with our own fight response. This is where children need to see a faith response the most. To put God's will and direction ahead of our inner desire to fight back with vengeance is a huge struggle. We need to strive to make a faith response something our children witness more often than a response stemming from our emotions. Our responses to the pushes and conflicts of life are not the only responses needing to be based in faith. We also need to address opportunities with a faith response. Not every good thing offered to us is good for us. So when the good offers come our way, whether these are personal, like a volunteer opportunity or a new relationship, or professional, like a job opportunity or promotion, we need to respond through faith and by listening to God's leading. This practice will be one of the most important skills you can model for your children. I have stepped away from several opportunities most would say were golden and amazing with only one reason for saying no, namely that I was not at peace with saying yes. God can speak to us by giving us peace about a situation that may run counter to conventional wisdom. But I am seeking divine wisdom, and so the peace that passes all understanding is what I seek.

> And the peace of God, which transcends all understanding, will guard your hearts and your minds in Christ Jesus. (Philippians 4:7 NIV)

Making decisions based in faith can be unsettling. Faith is a scary word! Acting in faith often runs counter to conventional wisdom. It can put us in frightening places. Acting in faith also puts us in God's will for our lives and leads us to fulfill the purpose we were created to fulfill.

And without faith it is impossible to please God, because anyone who comes to him must believe that he exists and that he rewards those who earnestly seek him. By faith Noah, when warned about things not yet seen, in holy fear built an ark to save his family. (Hebrews 11:6–7 NIV)

We read in Hebrews this reference to Noah and the faith he demonstrated as he built the ark. Clearly this was an act running against the conventional wisdom of the day. In fact, Noah was subjected to ridicule by his neighbors, but he acted in faith. The faith response of Noah put his sons in a position of decision. They watched as their father, living in a culture forsaking God, responded to God's direction to build the ark without hesitation. He followed God with integrity and would not compromise despite a culture compromising to the point of abandoning their faith. What a blessing Noah was to his sons. The way he lived his faith helped them make the decisions each of them faced in regard to living their own faith. How many times can your children identify your faith-based decisions, especially when they go against conventional and cultural norms? These are the modeling moments of faith-based responses our children need to see. They are scary and often can make us feel like we are building a huge boat in a place where a boat is not needed. But the leading of God outweighs the opinions on Facebook. Go in the direction God leads. Model faith-based responses in life so your children will have an example to imitate. Our lives as parents should convince those around us of the joy we gain by living our faith in our lives.

The faith-based responses we live model more for our children than just responses. When we step out in faith, even when it seems like we are going out on a limb, we model hope. We must hold hope for our future, as well as hope for the future of our children, in our hearts. Our children will gain a heart-deep understanding of hope from our faith-based responses to the challenges we face in life. I am certain that when Noah was building the ark, there were many questions in his head. But also, there was hope. He had hope that God was going to do what God had told him. He had hope his family would survive the flood.

When we step out in faith, we have questions in our hearts—but more than the questions, we have hope. Our children need to see hope in the watchtower. God didn't put us here to play it safe and to do the sure things. He calls us to build a giant boat in the desert. Isn't that what parenting is? We step out in faith and go against what the common conventions dictate. We are striving to raise faith-guided children with only one parent living in the household we live in. I know many times in these years I have felt like I was building a massive boat in a desert. The great part is, I have had the peace that passes understanding to guide me and hope to sustain me. Hope for tomorrow is a beautiful gift to model and give to your children. Hope for tomorrow gives us the ability to endure any struggle of today. I want my children to see hope in the watchtower!

I am thankful for the scriptures providing hope to support me. There are countless stories of faith responses and acts of faith to draw from for support. As I read about Noah, I get affirmation for doing what I need to do today so my children will be able to model my approach for themselves in the future. Noah didn't wait until the rain started to start building the boat. He started building it when he heard God's command to do so. Another great lesson from Noah's story is how he completely bought in to what God told him to do. He didn't try to keep his boat a secret or build a smaller version; he went all out in the direction God sent him. I want my children to see me demonstrate this type of committed faith response so they will also have that type of response. Noah also teaches me to let God be the keeper of times and seasons. In the story, Noah is not the one to start the rain, and Noah is not the one to shut the door on the ark—God does those things. If we allow scripture to support us, we will gain patience with the time lines that God establishes. Too often we want a door to open or close at the time of our choosing. God's timing is perfect and is often very different from our own. I have wondered why the timing of certain situations did or did not work out the way I would have planned. Then with the blessing of time and the view hindsight provides, I thank God for the divine timing I struggled to understand. When our children witness patience resulting from trusting God's timing, they will gain the ability to trust God's timing as well. Not only do we model patience as we trust God's timing, but also we model gratitude for the season we are living in now. There is no room in the watchtower for modeling the inability to be grateful for what we have in the moments of today. What do we teach our children if we are looking at our building project and complaining because the rain hasn't started yet? You know the type of thinking I am referring to—the *If I can just get past the terrible twos*, or *If I could just get a raise*, or *If I would just meet a person who would ...*, or *If I could just have a nicer house* type of thinking. There is no room in the watchtower for that kind of thinking. What your children need to see in the watchtower is gratitude for the moment. Right now, all around you are abundant sources of joy. Be thankful for the season you are living in now. It will not be permanent. It may be full of challenges and heartaches, but even in those you can see evidence of God's hand and find reasons for gratitude. When we demonstrate gratitude to our children, even in the hardest times, we model a reverence for God's timing and God's hand in our lives.

> Praise be to the God and Father of our Lord Jesus Christ, the Father of compassion and the God of all comfort, who comforts us in all our troubles, so that we can comfort those in any trouble with the comfort we ourselves receive from God. (2 Corinthians 1:3–4 NIV)

When we go to God with hope and gratitude, we place ourselves in his hands for comfort and help. We receive comfort from God and help in our moments of struggle so that we can continue to provide comfort, strength, and spiritual guidance to our children. Each time we turn to God as our source of compassion and comfort, we model for our children the practice of turning to God. God fills us again and again so that we can provide for our children what they truly need to gain: the habit of turning to God to meet their needs. As we seek comfort and guidance from God, we need to remember it may be God's redemptive work in those around us—or God's transformative work in those around us—keeping us in the place we struggle with today. God may not accomplish his work in others if the struggle we face is eliminated. It is a part of our reality that our time in the watchtower not only requires difficult self-examination and removal of the patterns we do not want our children to imitate but also involves difficult times of struggle. These times of struggle require a genuine faith response from us if we are to receive God's comfort and see what God is doing for us and through us. We may be praying for the struggle to end, but it may be that for God's purpose to be accomplished, he answers that prayer with no. Jesus wept in the garden of Gethsemane and asked that the responsibility of crucifixion be removed from him. God could not save the world and spare his Son. God's purpose of salvation could not be accomplished without Jesus going to the cross. While Jesus was praying and while the tears were fresh on his face, he also prayed, "Not my will but thine be done." Can you pray that? Are you willing to continue with your struggle or accept it if God's work in those around you can be accomplished best if you remain in your difficulty? Can you say through your tears "Thy will be done" if your difficulty or challenge will model faith responses and teach your children faith—or strengthen their faith walk and their trust in God? If your struggle remaining will in some way bring your children closer to being who God has made them to be, can you remain in the place where you pray "Thy will be done" through your tears?

As parents we will choose to do what is best for our children. For some of us, knowing that in God's hands our struggles can be what is best for our children will prevent us from seeking a reckless or hasty solution to the struggle. We don't enjoy struggles, and if it seems there is an easy solution, why not take it? Sometimes those self-made solutions only make bigger struggles in the long run. Model for your children the faith responses of prayer, patience, hope in God's work in your life, and allowing the peace that passes understanding to guard your heart and mind thus leading you in the direction God has planned for you. Most significantly for your endurance, realize your struggle could be a source of God's work in the lives of your children.

When I view the struggle I am facing from the perspective that my children are gaining faith to live out who God created them to be, my struggle gets smaller and my endurance and desire to respond with faith increases. I am willing to endure and even suffer for the faith gains of my children. I remind myself that they are more likely to face challenges in life with a faith response if I can endure and model faith responses for them instead of seeking a quick or easy self-directed solution. We single parents can use this type of perspective to decrease our worry about struggles we face and consistently turn the situations over to God for guidance and solutions. We need to strive to turn every area of our lives over to God's control. We can turn over our loneliness, fears, and feelings of defeat to God for guidance and solutions. We can seek God's guidance first in all the decisions about our children and the situations they face.

The benefit is not just for our children. We will gain strength in our faith, and faith gives us confident expectation. If God has called you to accomplish something, he will equip you to accomplish it and allow you to realize what you have been called to accomplish. If you know God has spoken a word to you, then trust it completely! Have confidence in that. Have hope. When you are facing impossible situations, know that God will do the impossible.

> Jesus replied, "What is impossible with man is possible with God." (Luke 18:27 NIV)

As we work to raise our children, we will face difficult circumstances and fierce opposition at times. Our response to this opposition will show our children how they should respond to the same. We will also have moments of failure—and so will our children. These also can be faced with a faith response of grace and forgiveness. And our successes and our children's successes should be faced with a faith response of gratitude and praise. Parenting, particularly single parenting, requires so many responses to our children and their needs and actions. For the purpose of modeling, and for our own success as parents, we need to seek God first and react as a parent after we have sought God's input. When we demonstrate asking and obeying, we are better parents. Equally as important, we model the behaviors of faith-guided people. When our children look up at the watchtower, we want them to see a faith-guided parent. Our time in the watchtower is only a season. Before we realize it, our children will have their own watchtowers. We need to stand watch over our children and embrace all the joy of the view.

> Train up a child in the way he should go, and even when he is old he will not depart from it. (Proverbs 22:6 RSV)

Messy Room, Messy Topic: Stewardship

Each of you should use whatever gift you have received to serve others, as faithful stewards of God's grace in its various forms.

—1 Peter 4:10 (NIV)

The most intense day I can recall in all my years as a parent happened when my children were very young. In keeping with the standard expectation, I told them to clean up their rooms and put their toys away. As my children were getting older, the number of toys was getting larger. As the number of toys grew, so did the size of the mess my children could make. When I checked on the cleaning progress, nothing had changed. The mess was still overtaking the room. I gave them a deadline, a specific amount of time to accomplish the cleanup. I gave them a fifteen-minute warning, a ten-minute warning, and then a five-minute warning. I could tell that very little cleaning was happening despite the warnings. Then it happened: time was up. I walked in with a large trash bag, and together we put all the toys that had not been cleaned up into the bag. I explained that if they had too many toys to take care of, we should give the toys to children who did not have any toys to play with at all. That is when the crying started. The crying continued while we drove to the collection site for the local outreach organization. The crying continued for most of the ride home. I think my children thought I was the most awful parent on the planet that day. To tell the truth, my heart was breaking and I was sick to my stomach the entire time. The crying did finally stop. But my stomach did not settle down, and I did not sleep well that night. My kids recovered much faster than I did. Most importantly, the lesson they learned has stayed with them.

They understand clearly that the blessings we enjoy are to be cared for, maintained, and treated with respect. Even into the teen years I have been able to ask, "So, do you have too many clothes to take care of?" The response is immediate and thorough as the clothes are put away and the room is straightened. We all can recognize that our culture is one that promotes material gain and that has taught a sense of entitlement to many. We need to rethink our position on this if we believe the only children affected by affluence are the children of the very wealthy. In my classroom I encounter students of almost every socioeconomic level, and I can honestly say that the entitlement attitude has made its way to children of all levels. The idea that they should have all they want, and that if something should be lost or damaged, it should be replaced without repercussion, prevails. The school lost and found overflows with expensive items that are rarely claimed. In several cases our school lost and found has included wallets with cash in them, more cash than most of the teachers have in their wallets. The students are not worried about these things; they know they will be replaced. This is not a mind-set that will promote successful living for those who are allowed to think like this. One task we must address as parents is teaching and modeling stewardship.

Most of us hear *stewardship* and think of that awkward and possibly offensive topic the pastor preaches on once a year—or perhaps twice a year. This is the sermon the pastor is clearly uncomfortable preaching and that usually causes the congregation to recoil. While that is a piece of the picture, it is not the whole picture. Yes, stewardship does involve the scriptural instruction to bring to God a tithe (this would be 10 percent) and an offering. The personal interpretation of 10 percent is between you and God. I am not going to enter into the debate of 10 percent of pretax or post tax income or ask if housing allowances factor in. That is for you to resolve with God through your own prayerful study of what the scripture is indicating. What is not open for debate is this: God is the giver of the blessings in our lives. We need to be thankful for all we are blessed with and give to God a tithe and an offering in return. This is something our children need to see us do so they understand that it is a part of a faithful gratitude response to God. If they never see us place our tithe and offering on the altar for God, it is likely they will not understand this as a part of their faith and personal relationship with God in their adult years.

But that act of worship is only one small part of the entire picture of stewardship. Teaching our children to be good stewards of all their blessings begins with teaching them to be grateful for all the blessings that surround them. Every year we have a canned food drive at the school where I teach to help the local outreach organization fill the food pantry. When the drive is announced, there is mild interest and enthusiasm. Then I share some general information with my students and change the interest level dramatically. I inform them there are children in our community who do not get to eat over the weekend because the meals they rely on are the school breakfasts and lunches. I ask them to think about this: *When you get home from school, if you are hungry, can you find something in your home to eat?* I remind them there are students who can't. At the start of the food drive there is little interest, but after my students realize the blessings they do have and that they could genuinely help others, the results are amazing. We simply need to make a habit of expressing our gratitude to God for all we have, and make sure we remind our children to be thankful as well. Too often we take for granted that we have to figure out what to make for dinner. We grumble because we have to make dinner. We need to change our thinking and be thankful that we have options and can decide what we will serve for dinner. We need to be thankful that we can make dinner for our family. A powerful sense of stewardship is rooted in a strong sense of gratitude!

As our children gain a greater sense of gratitude, we should teach them to be good stewards of all they are blessed with. This does mean taking care of the things they have, keeping them picked up and kept in reasonable order. Realize what you deem to be organized and that what seems organized to them may be very different. Allow them to establish organization within the boundaries of what is acceptable for your home. The important part is that they realize keeping things in order and taking care of things is a part of good stewardship. This is an area where parenting gets difficult. If children don't take care of the things they have, the amount needs to be reduced. When they lose things or carelessly break things, they need to earn a replacement, not just get a new one right away. Most of the things we are surrounded with are not necessities. While your child will say they are, we know the truth: that we live in an extremely affluent country, and most children are living with much more than they actually need for safety and survival. Gratitude will help them see that, and good stewardship practices will help them appreciate and maintain what they are blessed to own.

My daughter will identify very quickly what she calls "the worst summer of her life." It was the summer that began with her wrecking the car she was blessed to drive—that had my name on the title. She had just finished her first year of college, and her college savings account was empty. She was planning to get a job but hadn't found one yet. I speculate she was hoping for a fun and interesting job. Once the car incident occurred, looking for a job turned to desperately needing a job because she would be paying the insurance deductible for the needed repairs. Now facing a need to earn college money and insurance deductible money, she had to find a solution fast. As a result, she got to spend the summer waiting tables at a local restaurant. She had not hoped for a job waiting on tables. By the end of that summer she had a fresh perspective, a repaired car, and improved driving habits. I had a hard time watching her struggle through that summer, but I knew that the valuable lessons she was learning about her role as a steward of the things she is blessed to have around her would make it all worthwhile.

A significant part of teaching stewardship to our children is budgeting. We need to model for them strong financial responsibility. Establish a budget that is realistic and balanced and has room for emergency needs, and then live within that budget. If budgeting is not a skill you learned prior to now, learn it. It will make your household run smoothly and reduce your stress. A great way to learn this is to attend a program like Dave Ramsey's Financial Peace University, which is often taught through local churches. Other options for learning and gaining budgeting skill can be as easy as doing an online search for "how to budget my money." As an example of stewardship for your children, remember that the first item you place in the budget ledger is your tithe.

It is important your children grow up hearing phrases like "I budgeted and saved [this amount] for your prom dress," or "That will not fit in the budget this month; let me save for that," or "No, we are not getting that, because it is not on the grocery list this week and it is not needed." These types of phrases teach vital lessons to your children as well as help you maintain your budget. When you tell your children there is a specific amount of money saved for a special item, you accomplish several things. You teach them that one should set money aside and save for important things. You also empower them to begin to budget for themselves by establishing a spending limit for the special item they are about to choose. The first time I shared with my daughter the spending limit based on the amount of money I had saved for back-to-school clothes, she began to develop her sale-hunting and bargain-buying skill—a skill that is now refined and matured and serving her extremely well as she advances into adulthood. When your children hear that something doesn't fit into the budget and will have to be saved for and purchased later, they learn that things worth owning are worth working and saving for. They also gain perspective on the reason they should take care of the things they are blessed with. They will appreciate and care for things because they realize ownership takes time and effort. They will also learn and experience that just because they desire an item does not justify going over budget or getting in debt to have that item. When they hear the impulse item they picked up at the grocery store is not on the list and not needed, they will learn one of the foundational principles of living within a budget. They will learn that you plan ahead, that you have a specific set spending amount, and that the cart you are pushing is not a place to just load anything they want. If you think about it from a child's perspective, you go into a store, you choose what appears to them to be whatever you want, and then you get to take it all home. Why shouldn't they get to pick what they want? So make a list, and make sure they know there is a list. At the age when my children could reach for something that looked good to them, they would hear me say, "It's not on the list." As soon as they started going to school and carrying a lunch, I would ask them what they wanted in those lunches and what should be on the grocery list. Involve them in meal planning, grocery list construction, and all forms of budgeting and living within the budget. The exciting part of this is that as teens and adults, when a matter of budget becomes a crucial life skill, they will already be aware of and comfortable with the concept. I have watched my daughter move into adulthood with a clear budget sense, and thus far it is serving her extremely well. She will make sacrifices so she can protect her growing savings account. It makes every time she complained about not getting a "treat" at the grocery store worth it.

Some people back away from the word *budget* like it is indicative of a confinement that will ruin the happiness they currently have. I want to make it clear that a budget is the opposite. It frees your mind to focus on the joys around you and the relationships you enjoy with your children, instead of feeling anxiety over bills and costs that are a part of living. Gratitude is a key part of this. Gratitude opens our eyes to the joy and goodness we have, regardless of how much or how little we have. Keep gratitude at the foundation so the words you speak to your children are "That's not in the budget" instead of "I can't afford that" or "That costs too much." Having a budget and living within that budget is financially responsible and is part of living the life of a good steward. A budget does not imply having a large income or a small income. It implies good stewardship. Gratitude does not leave room for the "I don't have enough" attitude. It also protects us from the temptation to blame others for what seems to us like a shortfall of income. Gratitude will protect our children from those negative statements about others that will only hurt their hearts. Yes, I am talking about those who deal with another person in regard to child support and other financial matters. No one walks the road you do. Many people may walk similar paths, but we each have our own struggles and challenges. I recognize I do not know the details that cause financial challenges for every single parent. However, I do realize that some single parents deal with financial matters with another adult outside their home while others don't. I have encountered many sets of divorced parents in my years of teaching who have managed to put the children first and their hurts to the side. Those are impressive people who genuinely want their children not to suffer. Unfortunately I have encountered more people who do not keep the hearts of their children as the first obligation. They squander support payments, or fail to make adequate payments, or worse yet put the children in the middle by complaining to them about the payments. They refuse to pay for school lunches or other necessities because "that's what the payments should be going for," or "the payments can't cover that." I am not going to weigh in on how people deal with payments. I will say that watching a child go without lunch because of a parent's anger about how payments are handled is tragic. Listening to a group of teens talk about how their divorced parents complain to them about the other parent is tragic. Gratitude is the best prevention method for this. If adults would maintain an attitude of gratitude, then the need to complain would be reduced. When adults complain to children about a person the children love, the ones who suffer and get hurt the most are the children. No matter how tight the budget gets, refuse to allow your gratitude to decrease. In this way, you refuse to let your children suffer.

> Rejoice always, pray continually, give thanks in all circumstances; for this is God's will for you in Christ Jesus. (1 Thessalonians 5:16–18 NIV)

Remember, gratitude is the foundation of joy. There is great peace and freedom found in a grateful heart that is thankful for all the good you receive from God. This joy and peace has nothing to do with support payments or life insurance policies. It comes when we realize that God is providing what we need and we can be grateful for all that we have.

Stewardship is more than tithing; it is gratitude for the blessings we have and managing and caring for those blessings. It is passing that on to our children by our actions and example. As we are responsible with our spending and wise with our budgeting and financial approach, our children will learn to be the same. It does not take tremendous earnings to accomplish this. Stewardship can be done at any income level. It takes self-discipline and self-control to establish a budget that fits with your income and to live within that budget. There are lots of purchases I would like to make and lots of trips I would like to take, and my car has one hundred thousand miles on it. However, the lessons my children learn from my example of self-discipline and living within a budget that fits with my teaching salary are far too valuable to sacrifice. The added bonus of knowing my financial security is established and I don't have debt to worry about is a source of peace that I treasure.

Finances is not the only area where stewardship applies. We must teach our children through lessons and examples to be good stewards of their time, their energy, their talents, the tasks and work in front of them, and the ways they serve others. Stewardship of all we are given requires our ability to see that the most important things we have and are given are not financial. We have a limited amount of time and energy. I am sure I am not the only single parent who feels buried under the load of all that needs to be accomplished in the span of a day or a week. It can be overwhelming, and sometimes I want to give up and just lie down. But the fear that I might be buried under a pile of dirty laundry if I were to actually lie down for a few minutes prevents me from just stopping. Single parents are the masters of multitasking and doing more in one day than some people do in a week. I would recommend that you keep a schedule and teach it to your children. Allow them to see how you budget your time so they can learn to apply this skill to their own habits and lives. For each of us, what the actual schedule looks like will vary, but it is important that our children see there is a routine and a schedule that is used to prevent us from wasting valuable time.

When I attend a game to watch my child, I watch my child. I also take pictures and cheer. I am there to watch my child. Having a schedule allows me to live in the moment and embrace what my children are doing. I don't just sit through practices though. I take work to do, or get in a workout for myself, or run errands that need to be done. My children understand productivity is a necessity. They also understand that to be productive requires a plan—a schedule. So they know all the dirty clothes must be in the laundry room on Sunday evening when I start the washing machine. They know groceries will be purchased on Monday and that things they need should be added to the list before Monday afternoon. When my daughter was in high school, she started to exhibit how this had soaked into her way of thinking. She began keeping a color-coded planner with major projects planned out by the steps needed and with the date when each should be done so the project was completed on time.

My children will see me work tirelessly but will also see me intentionally spend time sitting with them and watching a movie, TV show, or game. By keeping a schedule in place, I can focus on the relaxing event instead of worrying about what might need to be done later. I have a schedule, and I know what needs to be done and when. This stewardship of time has been most beneficial when dealing with social media. I don't have time in my schedule to just scroll through a social media site. My time is budgeted, and scrolling through social media does not fit in the budgeted time. When my children start scrolling too much or too often, we discuss the budgeting of time and the amount of time spent. I don't usually have to go very far in the conversation before they will offer their own insight and express their realization that they can't afford to waste that much time on it. Time is such a valuable commodity. Once it is spent, we can't get it back. Budget your time to meet your children's needs, and make spending time with them your primary focus. It will not be long before you will not have this priority in your time budget. Be grateful that you have this priority while you do!

While budgeting your energy you need to be aware of the income sources and expenditures of energy you have in your life. Many people gain energy from quiet time, so they need to invest in daily quiet time. Others gain energy from exercise, so they need to invest in regular exercise. If you need some socializing to gain energy, then find ways to add social time into your schedule. Invest in your energy level so the income of energy is as high as possible. Examine the expenditures of energy as well, and eliminate what you can from your schedule just like you eliminate wasteful spending from your finances. If certain people or situations drain your energy, then remove those if they are not vital, or avoid them if possible. Protect your energy levels like you would any other asset.

Shortly after I was widowed I was speaking with a woman who was also widowed and had two children. We were talking about time demands and struggles. She made a simple recommendation—paper plates. For the few years that both her children were small and she was adjusting to the entire workload at the house, she said she used paper plates and cups. To reduce the demand on dishes that needed washing, this practice made sense to her. She felt that it took part of the load off her and saved some of her energy for her children. We need to discover what our own "paper plates" are when it comes to protecting our energy. Recognize that you have a finite amount of energy. What is spent on the needs of living daily is not available to be spent on your children.

Another aspect of stewardship is in the way we use our talents and perform the tasks in front of us. We need to teach our children that the talents they have are a gift from God and need to be protected and nurtured if they are to be developed. Additionally, children need to be responsible stewards of the work and tasks placed in their lives. It is easiest to teach all of these things by example. We need to be certain we are doing each task we take on with effort and to the best of our ability. I lack talent in the area of cooking. My children still see me put in effort when I attempt to cook dinner. I can't say they always eat a delicious dinner, but I can say they always see me making a genuine effort. My children also know that when I go to work, I am working hard and focused on my job. I do not bring work home on a regular basis. They know I work hard when I am there, and when I am not, I devote my time to them. I am trying to demonstrate for them and teach them to live in the moment, work hard in the areas of their talents, and give maximum effort to be a good steward of the talents God has given them. I want to help them recognize that their talents are from God and that they should invest in them. I can speak this, but if I live it as well, it will help them learn it. Additionally, they need to learn by experience that good stewardship of time and energy involves working hard on tasks they would not choose, such as homework and household chores. Teaching them to expend energy on these tasks as the first things done establishes healthy lifelong habits. Most children would not choose to do homework or simple household tasks. Children need to establish the habit of tending to these things up front, before their energy levels are drained. Additionally, it is good for them to learn that certain tasks are simply what are done to be a part of the family unit. Children need tasks that are expectations—not money-earning jobs, but simply tasks that are expected because they are a part of the family unit.

I accomplished this in my home by assigning certain jobs to each child. One child was responsible for rinsing dishes and loading the dishwasher. Another child was responsible for emptying the dishes from the dishwasher once it had run. Then it was my responsibility to establish a deadline but not a time line. Allow your children to budget time and either enjoy success when it works out well or suffer failure when it does not. I would alert my child that the dishes in the dishwasher were clean and then give a deadline of "by the end of the day." Sometimes, when wise budgeting of time is used, the dishes got unloaded early in the day. A few times procrastination was used instead of wise time management. Then at the end of the day when my child was tired, the dishwasher stood between that tired child and bed. That did not have to happen too often before my child learned valuable lessons about time and energy management and work management. The additional benefit of expected tasks is that a sense of responsibility toward the family begins to develop. It was a great day when my teen son just started taking the full trash bag out to the garage without my asking. He is not assigned this task. He has come to a greater awareness of the family unit as a whole, the needs of the family unit, and how he contributes to the family by taking care of tasks that need to be done when he sees them. That is the goal of assigning tasks as part of good work management stewardship.

It seems to go without saying that another aspect of task, talent, and time stewardship is approach to study habits and schoolwork. While children are school age, it is a natural part of stewardship for them to care about the quality and attend to the thoroughness of their work for school. Completion of all homework and classwork is the minimum expectation for those who are good stewards of their intellects. I am not implying that perfect grades are expected. My school experience clearly taught me that a student can give genuine effort and attention and still struggle with a concept. This was the case for me when I sat in math class and chemistry class. Hard work does not always result in perfect scores. In fact, in those subjects, hard work only resulted in my passing the class. We need to teach our children and hold them accountable for maximum effort, not top-of-the-class honor roll status.

We also need to teach our children to be good stewards of potential acts of service. We need to participate in service opportunities and help our children see this as a part of being a good steward of all we have been given. Some churches offer family mission trips. When your children reach the later teen years, they can participate in Habitat for Humanity build projects. Collecting items for local outreach and food bank organizations can introduce your child to acts of service. It is also important that they experience simple and personal acts of service such as taking a meal to a sick friend or helping a friend get some yard work done. Each year my children and I help a close friend hang Christmas lights on her house. These small acts impress upon your children the concept that if one is blessed with an ability to cook or to climb a ladder without fear, then as a good steward of that blessing, one give of oneself and that ability.

The greatest challenge for us as single parents is the struggle with multiple settings. If you are single parenting and there is another parent sharing custody, it would be ideal to work together and get on the same page with this concept. If that is not possible, then open honest communication with your children about the different styles of stewardship is a vital need. If you fail to communicate openly about the differences, you will invite a struggle for your children you do not want to allow. As a teacher, I get to see this from a unique and informative perspective. I hear the kids who are in these positions talk to their friends. They discuss the way one parent tries to outspend the other and how they know how to play the two adults against each other to get the monetary gain they are seeking. Regardless of your differences with the other parent of your children, you need to communicate honestly and openly with each other for the sake of your children. The angst you may or may not feel is not something that should affect children any more than they already have encountered.

Blended families and families with divorced parents need to be aware that if there are two different sets of rules, you establish an environment that generates the possibility of the children playing one set of rules against the other. Additionally, this teaches kids to get along on the surface and to look like they accept the rules. In reality they are learning far too well how to simply get along. They learn what looks right in two different settings, and they begin to lose track of what is genuinely right. This basically teaches them to do what they have to do just to get along. The clear problem here is that they learn to do whatever they have to do to get along, so when the "what you have to do to get along" with their peers turns into compromising their morals or doing things that are illegal or dangerous, they simply do what they have to do to get along. This makes it easy for them to get along with peers and be easily accepted by them, and it makes these children easy to have in either home. This is not a positive thing as children grow older and the cost of the compromise required to get along becomes greater. It is like the old saying goes: if you don't stand for something, you will fall for anything. We don't want this to be true of our children.

In every situation we need to choose what is best for our children regardless of the difficulty it generates for us. Too often I hear children say, "I know I can get away with this because my parents refuse to actually talk to each other. They will never figure it out." We need to deal with the difficult conversation, or even the confrontational conversation, to avoid our children learning how to manipulate, deceive, and succumb to a "whatever it takes to get along" approach to life. This is a part of our responsibility as good stewards of our children. It is hard to hear that we need to have confrontational or uncomfortable conversations to generate healthy environments for our children. Our children are worth it. From the teacher's perspective, I have heard the negative "They will never talk to each other" more times than I should have, but I have also heard the response on many occasions of "Oh well, my parents would let each other know, so I could never ..." Those are people who have put the children first and who have set the pains in their hearts aside to do what is best for their children. They have created a healthy set of homes. These are people who are working to be good stewards of the children they have been blessed to raise.

We have been blessed with treasures we call our children. We must be good stewards of them through what we teach them by design and by demonstration. Good stewardship is far more than a simple 10 percent.

GO AND MAKE DISCIPLES

Therefore go and make disciples of all nations, baptizing them in the name of the Father and of the Son and of the Holy Spirit.

—Matthew 28:19 (NIV)

How many times have we told our children "actions speak louder than words"? We say it because that saying is true. When Jesus tells us to go and make disciples, he is telling us we need to communicate our faith to those around us in words and in actions. If we are going to raise faith-directed children, they must also be able to communicate their faith to those around them through words and actions as well. We need to teach this to our children by living it in front of them. So much of living our faith can simply be summed up in Jesus's statement "Follow me." When Jesus calls disciples, he tells them, "Follow me." He doesn't command them, "Worship me." He wants us to show we are following him in our actions and in our daily living. When we show our commitment to our faith in our actions, then our words about our faith have depth and meaning. With depth and meaning, the joy of a life following Christ speaks to those who are searching, and the people who exhibit such joy can be used by God to make disciples. This is what we are commanded to accomplish as Christians and what we need to teach our children to seek to accomplish as well.

We also need to recognize that speeches without connections usually fall short of making a genuine impact. The times we are most touched by the words of others are when we are connected by relationship. The task of making disciples involves communicating and building relationships. To lead our children to a place where they can make disciples requires that they gain a strong sense of faith based in a deep belief that they are children of God, along with a strong skill in communication.

Teaching our children a strong skill in communication becomes more challenging with every new technological advance. Today our children are saturated with social media and device dependency. We need to teach our children how to build genuine and deep relationships that will generate real joy and allow others to hear them when they share the good news of Christ by words or by actions. Our children lack simple conversation skills, and in many cases, they lack the ability to look another person in the eye and communicate in a basic conversation. Social media has trained them to communicate in symbols, incomplete sentences, and snapshots. Many of our children are uncomfortable making a simple phone call. Most things can be accomplished by phone app, text, email, or online orders, and that is our children's comfort level. What can't be accomplished by text or email is the type of relationships we watched our parents have back in the day. Once upon a time people would chat with each other in the neighborhood. They would speak to each other at the store and when they saw each other in public. If someone had a family member who had been ill, people would ask how the person was doing. People knew what was going on in each other's lives, not in an intrusive way, but in a caring way. When a neighbor needed help or assistance in some way, others knew and would step up and help. This is the context that made living your faith and sharing your faith possible. People experienced compassion and care from one another; the example of Christ was evident. Today's children experience their parents posting things on Facebook, but to watch parents carry on a conversation is unusual. I am not a social media–based person. I speak with my friends and talk to people the old-fashioned way. I am always surprised when my children are embarrassed because I "talk so much" to others. My son will see me talking with a parent during his practice and is always concerned about why I was talking to the person and what was said. It seems strange to him that I would have a general casual conversation with a person. Teaching our children to engage in conversations and listen as others share is something we need to be intentional about doing. We need to understand that the social media culture does not nurture this. Additionally, we need to help them realize that a conversation is not an intrusion. Extending kindness is not an intrusion either.

When new neighbors moved in, I suggested to my children we make some brownies and then go over and give them to the new neighbors. My children were mortified! What a crazy thought. They could not imagine doing something that intrusive. When I was growing up, not to bake something and take it to the new neighbors would have mortified my mother. We need to realize that social media and the rules of social engagement have altered our children's perceptions of relationships and what is appropriate for establishing relationships. This can cripple our ability to allow others to see Christ in us on a daily basis through the way we live. Faith is more than a scripture under a picture on Instagram. A faith that makes disciples actively serves the needs of those around us. It is not just a blog with an inspirational thought. We can't expect our children to demonstrate and live out their faith to make disciples if we don't teach them to connect with others on a genuine level.

Ways to accomplish teaching relational skills begin with intentional approaches. Teach children to function device-free at certain times and in specific places. Dinner is a device-free zone in my home. Each of us simply leaves our phone facedown on the kitchen counter while we sit and eat. We don't eat for hours, so the messages, alerts, and emails can all wait while we actually talk to one another and share about the things going on in our lives. If conversation does not flow easily at first for you, start with a "question of the day" that everyone can talk about, or take a "share your good news from today" approach. Soon, conversation will flow and the need to prompt it will diminish.

My son practices his primary sport quite a distance from where we live. Early in the process of his sport development during our drives several days each week, we established a "deal." He gets to pick the radio station without my complaining, and in return, he will not put in earbuds or check his phone while we drive. We talk. Sometimes we talk about potential scientific inventions. Sometimes we talk about the way his heart aches over the decisions his friends are making. It doesn't matter what we talk about; I treasure the conversations that have allowed me to know who my son is, how he thinks, what hurts his heart, and what brings him joy and excitement. I am so thankful that our car is a device-free zone. Not to mention, my middle school students think I am so cool because I am knowledgeable about all the latest music artists and trends. That is an added bonus. When people comment about how much of a struggle it must be to keep doing the long drive so many days a week, I tell them, "I will really miss these drives someday." These are priceless hours in the car!

As my daughter became old enough to date, she would get comments regularly about how unusual it was that she would put her phone away and leave it in her purse during her dates. To her, a device-free setting seemed natural and respectful. For so many young men, a device-free date is a rare occasion. We need to teach our children a different way of managing the assault of input they encounter daily so they can learn to communicate and establish relationships that are the foundation for sharing the good news of Christ.

Establish device-free zones or settings, and enforce them. It will benefit your children in many ways. It will allow them to look up and enjoy the beauty of the world around them and meet the people who cross their paths each day face-to-face. It will empower communication between you and your children. Most importantly, it will enable them to speak the joy of life as a child of God to those who come to recognize this by the way they live.

Other communication skills are vital to living out a witness that will encourage discipleship in others. Teaching your children to communicate respectfully with authority figures is a basic skill you can't assume your children will gain through daily life. You need to guide them in this area. Teach them to use respectful terms when addressing coaches and teachers. These can vary based on geography, but respect is not geographical. A "yes, sir" or "yes, ma'am" is generally expected in certain areas. Addressing an adult with "Mister" or "Misses" or "Ms." should be expected regardless of the location. Treating others with respect has a significant effect on the respect others will give your children. As parents, we need to make an intentional effort to teach our children how to ask respectful questions, give respectful responses, and generate respectful communications. Practicing how to phrase a question is important. Teaching them to use the "I" message approach is very valuable: "I would like to improve on ..." or "I am not clear on your expectation of ..." are modes of questions that avoid disrespectful misinterpretations. Often I spoke through conversations with my children and shared feedback that helped them gain skill in this area. This does require that we as parents seek to see situations from the perspective of the adult our children will be speaking with, and not from the perspective of a protective parent who may not agree with what we are seeing. If I had a dollar for every time one of my children dealt with disappointment or decisions from an adult I could not understand, I would be a wealthy woman. The fact is, they gained more from learning to communicate respectfully and ask questions than they might have gained from those situations starting out in their favor.

One of the most important aspects of this life skill is teaching your children to pray before they speak. When facing a conversation with an authority figure, taking a moment to pray for God to guide their words and their thoughts is a practice that will not fail your children. The practice of praying with your children before they go into the situation is a great way to model this for them. If your children are seeking God's guidance as they approach authority figures with respect, this is a powerful witness to others who are watching!

In addition to respect for authorities, a humble attitude saturated with gratitude is very impactful. Each year teaching I will have one or two students who will thank me at the end of class every day. They genuinely endear themselves to me by simply demonstrating sincere thankfulness for the energy and effort I put into teaching class. These students are a witness to the goodness of God by simply expressing gratitude daily. Teach your children to thank their teachers and coaches. This is not always smooth or easy. There were numerous times when I would start toward the car with one of my children after a lesson or practice and ask if they had thanked the instructor or coach. If they answered no, we would stop walking and I would send them back to the field to thank the adult who had given them their time. Eventually, to avoid having to go back, my children developed the habit of saying thank you. It is rare to hear anyone say they are bothered by people expressing gratitude. We all appreciate gratitude, and therefore, expressing gratitude is foundational to respect. A simple thank-you makes a tremendous impact.

Gratitude expressed, even if out of habit or direction, eventually grows into an attitude of thankfulness that feels normal to your child.

When we express gratitude, it does not change the person we are thanking—he or she has already blessed us—it changes us. Expressing gratitude solidifies and secures our healthy sense of gratitude deep within. Thanking a teacher or coach helps our children realize that those who are instructing and teaching are consistently giving the best they have to offer each time they are working. That should not be taken for granted. Teaching our children to recognize that the many blessings they encounter each day are not owed to them is an important place to begin when helping them develop gratitude. The more we develop gratitude in our children, the stronger their witness will become.

Gratitude has an opposite. The opposite of gratitude is selfishness. Gratitude is based in a clear understanding that all we have are undeserved blessings. God has filled our lives with so many reasons for gratitude. To remain aware of the abundant blessings we enjoy will provide a mind-set that cancels out selfishness and provides the open heart that will be filled with the fruits of the Spirit and will naturally spread the good news of the Gospel.

Additionally, when we keep our minds focused on the goodness of God and all we have to be grateful for, the joy in our faith abounds. Joy gives our witness impact. More than that, joy is not circumstance driven. We will have joy in any circumstance. Genuine divine joy, not reliant upon circumstance, is powerful and can make disciples in the most unlikely of circumstances. In Acts 16, beginning with verse 16, we read of a situation like this. Paul and Silas are beaten and imprisoned, and yet they are praying and singing hymns. I personally think that would be a difficult thing to do. They had been flogged and shackled, and they were singing praises to God. In the end, the guard is converted to Christianity. This is what we are called to accomplish.

While it seems impossible, expressing gratitude in all circumstances is the starting point for us to praise God regardless of our circumstances. We need to make note of the fact that while in prison Paul and Silas were singing and others were listening. Too often we assume no one will hear and no one will be listening. We need to nurture gratitude so that in the most unlikely places, when we don't even realize someone is listening, what is heard from us and from our children is praise. This is the most effective way to make disciples of others.

We are children of God—that brings joy! We can't let our joy be determined by our circumstances. We can't allow our joy to be determined by our cultural standards. We can't allow the actions of others to determine our joy either. Our status as children of God is joy enough! When we choose joy in that manner, we become witnesses to those around us of the joy God generates and the gratitude we as Christians naturally hold in our hearts. This is a profound way of living, one that will not come naturally to our children. We must teach it purposefully, and the first lesson in that teaching is gratitude.

We need to personally be on guard so that society and culture do not rob us of the joy of life God wants for us. As your children move into the teen years, they become self-conscious and afraid to express joy openly. They want to still find joy in the simple things and feel gratitude for all the blessings they experience, but the world will try to convince them that fulfillment comes from what the world has to offer—acclaim, wealth, career advancement, fluid moral standards, and shallow relationships. Without direction and intentional teaching, they will easily succumb to that "ideal." Your intentional teaching otherwise will be the reason they can hold to their faith and live the abundant joy God intended for them. We need to teach our children not to settle for anything less than what God intends for them. We need to purposefully teach them to see clearly what the world has to offer and to respond to the joy God is offering with gratitude.

In addition to gratitude, we need to teach our children to embrace service. Our acts of service will do as much for making disciples as our words. In education we often use a phrase that clearly fits here: "they won't care about what you know until they know that you care." Service clearly communicates that we care. Involve your children in acts of service along with you, and show them the joy service can bring to those you serve and to your heart.

Too often we think our children are not capable of service because they are too young or too weak, but we are wrong. You can teach your children to serve others at a very early age. When I coach soccer, I play better. It's funny, but the return to the basics through teaching makes my basics improve. I have found in the classroom, when a student is shaky on a skill, I will ask that student to teach it to others. Through the experience of teaching it, the student gains confidence and strength in the skill. In the end, the student benefits as much or more than the one who was receiving the instruction.

I think serving others and sharing our faith has the same result. We gain strength and confidence in our faith as we share it with others through actions and words. Age and skill set is not an issue. It is in moments of service that we feel the abundant joy scripture tells us God wants for us. It is in service that others experience the agape love of God that speaks volumes more than any sermon or witness speech could ever impart.

Acts of service don't have to be grand adventuresome mission trips. The acts of service that will make disciples in your community are the acts of service needed in your community. Simple acts of giving and serving can be a profound witness. Teaching your children to see the situations around them and extend service when they see these situations is a tremendous step toward equipping them to make disciples. Hanging Christmas lights every year for a widowed mother of two, taking cookies to the fire station on Father's Day, filling a bag of groceries for the food pantry, and visiting a nursing home are examples of this type of service within your community that can spread agape love to those near you.

As a part of service to others, demonstrate for your children the importance of grace and unconditional love. The witness they will share with others as they seek to live out the call to make disciples will be enriched by their experiences with your demonstrations of grace and unconditional love. As your child experiences these from you, the reality of God's grace and unconditional love becomes clear. As your children experience this, they can then share it so others will experience it as well.

Other experiences that will enrich the witness your children can share will be through God-directed situations and the people God brings into your children's lives. When you see these, you need to teach your children to recognize them too. God leads us to places and situations we would never imagine, and puts people in our lives to impart wisdom and guidance we would not know to seek out for ourselves. When we realize we are in a situation that is God directed, we need to point it out to our children and work to teach them to see these situations as well. When we realize God has led people into our lives, or into the lives of our children, for our benefit, we need to point this out to our children so they can learn to see these blessings for themselves. Additionally, we need to teach them to discern the promptings of the Holy Spirit. The times we feel directed or led to act or speak are important lessons for our children, teaching them to follow those promptings as well. We must let our children watch and learn as we seek to live out the directions God sends us, so they will do the same. To simply expect that they will make disciples because they are disciples is not reasonable. We need to live out that calling, and we need to teach them how we are living out that calling. We need to be intentional in the ways we model and in the ways we teach discipleship so our children will have a skill set to employ on a daily basis.

The greatest joy of discipleship is being in constant company of God and walking daily with him. We can show this joy to our children and teach them through modelling what they should value most. We don't have to be concerned about where we are going or what we will accomplish if our primary concern is that we are walking where God leads us. This is how we model discipleship and how our children will effectively model it for those around them.

Not all our modeling will be a strong witness. We need to be honest with ourselves about the things in our lives that diminish or compromise our witness. We don't do our children any favors by acting as though our witness is spotless. If we could have a spotless witness, we wouldn't need grace. When we are honest with ourselves about our failings, we teach our children to be honest with themselves as well. This is where growth begins: in honest self-assessment. We will not only give our children a solid understanding of the value of grace but also empower them to grow in their discipleship.

Our job as parents is to share the good news about Jesus. The most effective way to accomplish this is to demonstrate the love of Christ until that love has won those around us to a relationship with Christ. We can demonstrate this to our children, and we can empower them to demonstrate Christ's love to those around them. They will only need to live out the love Christ has put in their hearts, and God will generate the transformation of those who experience that love into disciples.

We think we should raise our children to be accomplished professionals—doctors, lawyers, scientists, and so many other titles. Really, we need to be about raising our children to be disciples and teach them to go out and make disciples. That is what we are told to do.

Content in All Circumstances, Even Single Parenting—Ask Paul

---◈---

Grace and peace to you from God our Father and the
Lord Jesus Christ

—Galatians 1:3 (NIV)

Paul wrote many letters instructing churches and new followers. He intended to support the followers of Jesus in their individual faith journeys and the community of faithful followers as they learned to grow in faith with each other. He did not specifically write letters to single parents, but he did provide instruction and information by example that is valuable for us.

In Paul's writings we find he often refers to the thorn in his flesh. He does not provide detail about what that thorn is. I find this to be a blessing for my own faith journey. It is so much of a blessing that I often reflect on the intentional omission of that detail and how God knew I would need to be able to connect specifically to that struggle. I know I have my own weaknesses that are my own thorns in my flesh. I take comfort from and find guidance in knowing that the apostle Paul had struggles, and yet Paul provides scriptural guidance for my journey and growth as I deal with my own thorns.

Paul's nonspecific thorn in his flesh becomes universal—"a thorn"— and by lack of detail, it speaks to each of us and our own struggle. God provides for each of us the opportunity to specifically and individually identify with the struggle Paul wrote about. Every believer has dealt with a thorn at one time or another. I do think as single parents, we have greater opportunities to pick up thorns in our everyday lives. We all have weaknesses that cause us to be less than we want to be for God and less than we want to be for our children. Paul's life is an example and a guide on our journey because so many of his experiences are easily connected with so many of our circumstances. Paul provides an example resonating with our day-to-day living and giving us hope. We struggle and connect with his "thorn in the flesh" so well.

Paul, once Saul, had known wealth and social status. He had all the worldly gain defining success. Then he experienced the opposite. He lived through temporary blindness, life-altering changes of heart and mind, loss of status, shipwreck, persecution, imprisonment, and a host of situations we could not imagine surviving. Not only does Paul experience these, but also he praises God through them, witnesses to others, continues to convert Christians, and above all else speaks of being content in all of these dismal circumstances. This is why I find Paul to be the instructor of basic single-parenting approaches.

> I was given a thorn in my flesh, a messenger of Satan, to torment me. Three times I pleaded with the Lord to take it away from me. But he said to me, "My grace is sufficient for you, for my power is made perfect in weakness." Therefore I will boast all the more gladly about my weaknesses, so that Christ's power may rest on me. (2 Corinthians 12:7b–9 NIV)

I must be honest and reveal that when I read this scripture I feel that I, more than anyone I have ever met, am in the best position to boast. I can boast of so many weaknesses! There is so much of Christ's power resting on me! As I look at Paul and consider all he went through, I often think that his words about a thorn in his flesh, and peace and contentment in all circumstances, must have been written for those of us who struggle and suffer and still must go forward seeking to be faithful followers of Christ. I gain comfort and guidance as I relate Paul's experiences to those in my life and the lives of many single parents.

I know I have prayed for my thorns to be removed. Some have been removed, and others I know are still in place to glorify God's strength and power through my weaknesses. Knowing that God says "My power is sufficient for you" brings incredible hope and confidence when I feel too weak to face the challenges in front of me. An examination of some of the circumstances Paul endured produces many modern-day equivalents of circumstances common to single parenting. We all connect with the thorn in the flesh Paul writes about. This is only a start. When we look at Paul, we can all connect with many other situations and experiences and find hope and guidance for our own journey. Some of these experiences are as follows:

Testifying before kings – This is equivalent to situations where you must step up for your children and defend what they genuinely need. We are called to testify in situations like meetings with teachers to secure accommodations for learning differences, and meetings with the coach when your child has been treated unfairly. If you are blessed with a successful child, you face the challenge to remain humble and allow the life you live to testify to God's overwhelming blessing in your life. Paul kept the glory of God first in all he did, and this led to the opportunity to testify to the goodness of God.

Suffering persecution – Regardless of how you became a single parent, the sense of persecution is real. I have had so many small moments that caused me to feel persecuted. Most vivid in my memory was a formal dinner I was to attend shortly after I was widowed. The banquet tables were designed to have eight people at a table, but I was seated alone. The organizers simply left the seat next to mine empty because I messed up the table balance. That was a long and difficult evening, sitting with an unused place setting beside me. I recall the many times I have been told, "We didn't invite you because it was a couple's thing and we thought you would feel awkward." When I was singled, I experienced a definite loss of social status, friends, groups, and even the handy even number for the formal dinner table.

Speaking to large crowds – There are very few people in the world who truly enjoy speaking to large groups. In fact, there are even groups you can join to help you gain confidence and skill in this area. As a single parent, the way you live each day is speaking an entire sermon about selflessness and unconditional love to all those who are watching you and your children. There are times when we are called upon to speak out about the priorities we maintain for the sake of our children. If I had a dollar for every time I was asked "So are you dating?" I would have an entire vacation fund built up! Those people are pulling me on to a stage where I am expected to speak, regardless of my willingness.

In addition, there are times when your child is the focus of attention, sometimes positive and sometimes not so positive, and you suddenly are pushed to the front. How you act or react will speak volumes. Times when your child steals the show in the dance recital, or the school play, or a musical production, or the time when your child is the basketball player who draws the technical foul, are just a few of these moments. We have all had these moments—moments when we feel all eyes turn to us because of what our child has just accomplished or what our child has just done, and in that moment, we must speak to the large crowd looking our way and demonstrate humility, God's grace, and unconditional love. These are situations we have all experienced.

Starting up new churches – Paul started new churches in many different places. I am certain if you asked Saul what his five-, ten-, and fifteen-year career and life goals involved, being struck blind, being converted, and traveling abroad starting churches would not have been included. Once Saul became Paul, he went to places that were not in his plans. I know that once I was singled, I went to many places I had not planned on going. I have supported my children in many adventures I did not design. I have taken on jobs I would not have imagined. As a single parent, the greatest skill I have learned is that of going where God leads and doing what God calls me to do. It was from these very locations that Paul wrote about contentment. I am so thankful that as we go places we did not plan, experience new places to live, take on new jobs, and deal with new social settings, we can hold on to Paul's words about contentment because we know that, just like Paul, we are not going without God.

Performing miracles – Paul performed miracles in the name of Christ. We are also often called upon to accomplish miracles. How is this for a miracle: work a full-time job, run the household and do all the needed maintenance, buy groceries, pack lunches, help with the science project, tutor math you don't remember learning, take your kids to all the practices they need to attend, do laundry, make meals, clean up the kitchen, make any needed appointments, and get the kids to bed in time to get a good night of rest—and do that all in one day while keeping a positive attitude. Only by the power of God, showing strength in my weaknesses, is it possible for a day to look like this. Our days seem to look like this more often than not. God's power is the source of all miracles, and we are performing miracles daily by the strength of God. I know too often I neglect to thank God for the miracle that is the day I have just lived and the provisions that were put in place for my children.

Being stoned or whipped – Paul suffered tremendous physical attack. While most single parents have not been stoned by a crowd, we have experienced physical and emotional devastation. Most of us can identify a time when our disappointment and situation was actually causing so much emotional pain that it felt physical. Unfortunately we know many who have suffered physical abuse at the hands of a former spouse as well. Some of us have suffered at times when a former spouse found an unnecessary reason to take us back to court again, or when we got the letter from the government pronouncing that our marriage was "ended by death." I will never forget the actual physical pain I felt when I read the letter from the government telling me that my marriage was "ended by death" and that I needed to file my taxes as a single person. I felt like I had been physically attacked. I have been told the same feelings came with divorce papers being served and signing them. Yet Paul reminds us in these moments that we can still feel God's peace. The peace that passes understanding is something Paul speaks of convincingly. I can confidently say I have felt that peace in some incredibly difficult and painful moments.

Being shipwrecked – Being divorced, being widowed, losing a job, experiencing a death in the family, enduring financial struggles, suffering illness, being forced to move. These are only a few of the shipwreck moments we endure. Paul didn't want to be on the ship that sank any more than we want to be single parents. Paul listened to God, followed the leading he received, and survived. The important lesson in this for us is that we can survive our shipwreck as well. Be courageous because God is with you. And even if your ship is in pieces, you can hold on to those pieces and float to safety when you don't have the energy left to swim.

Being mocked – When Paul was Saul, he enjoyed social status and respect. Later he was mocked and had no social status. Our situation is closely connected to his. I have felt mocked on more occasions than I can count. The times when my children made well-meaning statements like "You dress so frumpy" and "Oh no, Mom, don't say that," or even when I was told, "Don't use emojis when you text because old people just shouldn't," were all moments when I certainly felt mocked. One of my all-time best was when my children had discussed why I never got asked out on dates, and one came to share with me the list of reasons why he felt I was not getting dates. I am sure it is perfectly normal to feel mocked when your child tells you that you are embarrassing her, so please just drop her off around the corner so no one sees you. I know we can all relate to the myriad of times when our ideas were dismissed or rejected, and then another adult said the same thing, exactly the same thing, and that adult was seen as amazing and wise. Paul endured mocking and counted all those occasions as opportunities for God's strength to shine. We can do the same.

Being conspired against – Paul knew what it was to have people around him set him up, manipulate circumstances, and conspire against him. Through those times, Paul continued to witness to the love and grace of Christ. We have found in our darkest hours those friends who turn out to be self-serving or manipulative, the kind who would *not* pull you out of a burning building. We have also known those who experience the other parent of their children putting those children in the middle of a vindictive and emotionally unhealthy situation. We know children have been played like pawns in the vindictive plans one parent has against the other, with innocent children being unknowingly placed in the middle of the dispute. We as single parents deal with those who conspire against us. Just like Paul, we can continue to witness to the love and grace of Christ and focus on the many wonderful people God places in our lives to nurture us, support us, and give us confidence to face the next day.

Being imprisoned – There are many times we would like to do something for ourselves, or something that would be fun, but we simply can't. Our budget and our time schedules just simply will not allow for it to happen. I have often felt connected to Paul as he sat in a prison cell, feeling like I would never be set free. I must remind myself that Paul used that time to praise God. When I feel down, defeated, and imprisoned,

I sing praise songs. You can't stay defeated and hopeless when you are singing praises to God. Scripture tells us that those who heard Paul's praises were converted. If you knew for certain that you would bring someone to Christ by singing a praise song today, you would sing! It would not matter how trapped you felt, you would sing. So do just that. Sing boldly, and know that whoever hears you will be blessed.

We can clearly identify with Paul and connect many of our feelings and circumstances to the life of Paul and the lessons we gain from his example. Most importantly, we need to constantly remind ourselves that Paul said in all circumstances he could be content. A great part of Paul's contentment came through his obedience to God. Paul went where God sent him and did what God asked of him. He took the assignment from God and completed the task. God's assignment for us is clear—we are to raise his children to be disciples and to become who he created them to be. In keeping God's assignment as our priority, in our obedience to God's task set in front of us, we can have the same contentment. There is possibly no other lesson we can model and teach our children with greater lasting value than the lesson of the deep contentment found in obedience to God.

Living this obedience to God and raising children with our relationship with God at the top of our priority list will bring both wonderful moments and hard moments. In 2 Corinthians 11:23–28 God revealed his plan for Paul. The vision involved the excitement of speaking before kings and large crowds, performing miracles, and starting churches. It also involved being stoned, imprisoned, and shipwrecked. This is the Paul who wrote, "I have learned to be content in all circumstances." This is the Paul whom we can connect with and relate to on so many levels. We realize that raising kids is a lot like the life of Paul, and doing it alone is even more like that. There are outpourings-of-love moments when your kids see what you do for them and thank you. They do sweet things and make you cards and try to cook you breakfast. It's like having all the joy and miracles and large crowds applauding. Of course there are also the times when they are defiant, moody, and rebellious, and you feel like you are being stoned to death by the glares of teenage eyes. There are also the times when you must exact discipline and you are left feeling shipwrecked. Other challenges come when you must make decisions for them to ensure the best possible outcome occurs, for example, the decision to change schools, your making them go to a set of driver's education classes instead of taking the easier online course, or your insistence that they take the more challenging academic courses. When your child doesn't like your decision, you feel isolated and imprisoned.

Can we take both sides and not complain? Can we be like Paul and say we are content in all circumstances? Can we also avoid comparing our situation and our children to what we see around us? I know that on the evenings when I am so tired and there is still a mountain of laundry and several burned-out light bulbs to change, it is tempting to look at the neighbor who has a husband to change the light bulbs and compare myself to her. I must spend my energy looking at the blessings God has given me. I must keep my eyes fixed on Jesus! Comparisons lead to discontentment, and I can't afford to go there. If I allow discontentment to take root in my thinking, I can grow a massive crop very quickly. As a parent, thankfulness for the blessings I enjoy must be what I demonstrate to my children. If I compare and become discontent, I will demonstrate all the wrong attitudes to my children. I can't afford to demonstrate negativity. We can't afford to demonstrate discontentment to our children.

We need to keep our eyes on the vision God has given us and on Jesus as our guide. That is what we need to be demonstrating to our children. When we model this attitude for our children, we will teach them to do the same. That is the assignment we have been given by God.

Comparing opens the door for another danger many single parents face. The opportunity for children to gain personal advantage by playing one parent against another is present only when we compare. We have all seen this accomplished at some point in some setting. Children of divorced parents who learn how a perfectly placed "Well, at Mom's, we …" can generate the end result they desire. The opportunity for this to work requires a parent who is willing to compare and allow his or her children to compare. If looking at how others do things and what others have is not a part of your thinking, the end result is an inability for this struggle to succeed. Once a child realizes that a luxury at one house and not another is simply how things are, playing it against the other parent is pointless. Your child will not gain anything from that approach other than the lesson of contentment with what God has provided.

Living in a genuine state of contentment with where you are and what you have because you know God is the center of your home and family generates wonderful strength for you as a parent. The ability not to compare and then not become discontent is one of the gains. Another gain is the ability to remain consistent with discipline and structure.

One day I was talking with a single parent who was sharing her fear of disciplining her children because she feared that her children might decide to live with the other parent who is out of state if she were to discipline them. For the sake of your children, and the ability to parent from a state of contentment and God-centeredness, these practical situations need to be addressed in a reasonable manner, focused on what is best for the children. In this particular situation, the two divorced parents living in different states needed to agree that the children should not look at a change of living location except between school years. This type of agreement gives the parent the comfort to establish rules and discipline to serve the best interests of the children. Rules can be established for an academic year without concern about the children deciding to move to another state. Children need stability, consistent discipline, and structure, and not a life of ease and omnipresent happy days.

From a study published on BusinessInsider.com I read the following very interesting findings. Parents of successful kids have these things in common:

- They make kids do chores—regular responsibilities around the home as a part of family responsibility. These things are as simple as being responsible for taking out the trash or making sure the dishes are done.

- They have high expectations for their children. They don't allow them to be less than their abilities allow. This entails doing simple things like expecting all homework assignments are completed on time and establishing consequences when this isn't accomplished. High expectations need to be clearly communicated, realistic, and partnered with responses. When the expectations are met, children need to feel the positive results, and if they fail to meet those expectations, they need to recognize negative results.

- They teach social skills at an early age; basic use of "please" and "thank you" and teaching concepts of sharing and community are a part of this. This should not stop as children grow up. While the children are growing up, these successful parents continue to teach basic social skills and awareness of others.

- They have healthy relationships with each other. If you are divorced, that does not mean you can't have a healthy relationship with your children's other parent. Putting your children first and your hurt second, along with a lot of prayer, can provide the foundation for a healthy relationship based on working together to accomplish what is best for your children. While the genuine hurt causing the divorce to have occurred may continue to cause you to want to speak ill of your former spouse, a healthy relationship between his or her two parents is a component of your child's success in the future. If you are widowed, establish healthy friendships and friendships with couples who have healthy marriages so your children can witness healthy relationships. Be aware of how you speak of your deceased spouse. Your children do not need to hear of the shortcomings of the parent they have lost.

- They have attained higher education. Sometimes situations have not put people in the place to accomplish this. Teaching your children to value learning and discovery is at the core of this. Demonstrate to your children a willingness to discover and learn new things. The modeling of learning for the joy of discovery is extremely valuable for your children.

- They teach math at an early age. This does not mean that you have to be a math expert. There are wonderful games and resources that can introduce math and spatial reasoning to young children.

- They are purposeful in building the relationship between themselves and their children.

- They are less stressed. This seems impossible for a single parent. The truth is, if we keep God at the center of our home and prayer as the first response to the challenges we face, we will feel less stress. We will not face fewer challenges, but we will face them with God at our side and less stress in our homes.

- They value effort over avoiding failure. Our society has come to a place where winning and being the best needs to be a guarantee. When my son was young I watched as parents took their boys to tryouts for highly competitive sports teams. I actually heard one mom say if her nine-year-old son could not make a top team, he needed to quit the sport. This is not what guarantees success. Allowing your child to fail, learn from it, and gain strength to make another attempt is far more valuable for a successful future than ensuring that he or she never experiences failure or loss.

These findings are significantly helpful for single parents trying to give their children the same opportunities for success as the kids who have both parents in a committed relationship in one home. I can't change the fact that my children lost their dad, but I can put these pieces in place in our home and hopefully provide a foundation for success for my children. I know that when my children were grieving the loss of their dad, I wanted to prevent them from hurting, so I didn't discipline them as I should have. I know when I wanted to say no to my children, I feared that they were already deprived due to a lack of a dad in the house, so I was not as restrictive as I should have been. This is a mistake I have made that you do not have to make. If I am content in my circumstance, then I will not fail to discipline my children because our circumstance is not like the neighbors'. Children need to hear no. Children need to have expectations of tasks and duties around the house. Children need to hear that the schedule is full. Children need to hear "that doesn't fit in the budget." I felt guilt when I heard my kids talk about the fantastic home-cooked meals their friends' mothers prepared or the amount of time other moms donated to the PTA. That guilt would lead me to indulge them in ways that were not in their best interests. My reality was that I had the role of the only income provider in the household. I felt guilt over that role instead of realizing God had blessed me with a wonderful job and feeling the contentment Paul speaks of.

After many years as a working mom, I read a study finding that the children of working moms usually stayed in school longer, were more likely to obtain jobs with supervisory roles, and often earned more than their peers who were raised by stay-at-home moms. I don't recall the source of that study or the years, so it may well be outdated information. The validity of the information is not the point. The point is, if I spend my energy being thankful for the blessings from God of a good job, and if I remain content with the income and home we are blessed to enjoy, my children will live in a healthy and less stressed environment. They are more likely to learn to value the contentment of living in God's will, and that is the greatest lesson I can teach. That is why it is vital to learn from Paul and be able to say, "I can be content in all circumstances."

THINK ON THESE THINGS

Finally, brothers and sisters, whatever is true, whatever
is noble, whatever is right, whatever is pure, whatever is
lovely, whatever is admirable—if anything is excellent
of praiseworthy—think about such things.

—Philippians 4:8 (NIV)

I grew up in a state that is rich in Native American Indian history. I
remember hearing a wonderful old teaching when I was young that
came from the Native American tradition. The teaching is about two
wolves. One wolf represents good, and the other represents evil. The
question is presented: which wolf will win in a fight? The answer is
this: the one you have fed. It is a simple truth. What you feed becomes
stronger. You become what you focus on. What you feed with attention
and concentration becomes dominant. This is why we must attend
to what our children think about and how they are entertained. We
must guard what they see and immerse themselves in. We spend so
much time, energy, and money on healthy food and good nutrition,
academic strength, physical strength and fitness, and the best clubs and
connections, but we completely disregard what wolf they are feeding. We
should start by tending to what wolf they feed in the form of psychological
health and not fool ourselves into believing this doesn't matter.

How much do we concern ourselves with the intake of our children's
minds? To be physically strong and healthy we must watch what we eat
and make sure we get exercise. It certainly stands to reason that we need
to tend to the health of our minds and hearts with the same diligence.
Where our minds wander in unguarded or idle moments reflects the
health of our minds as well as the health of our spirituality. If we have

fed the negative and evil wolf, evil will emerge in those idle moments. If our minds are not on positive and healthy thoughts, then they are causing deterioration of our spiritual strength. We must make a choice about what wolf we are feeding. We can keep God at the center of our thinking, or we can keep the negative there. It is a choice we need to make and one we need to guide our children in making as well.

It is not a choice we can ignore. The human mind is not something that can be placed in neutral. When I am in the car, I can put the car in drive or in reverse. There is also the option of neutral. Neutral is not really neutral. If I am on a hill or even a slight slope and I put the car in neutral and take my foot off the brake, the car is not going to stay in the same place. It will roll. Our thoughts are the same. We can either put them in drive toward God or put them in reverse and damage our connection with God. If we think we are in neutral, we are fooling ourselves. The same is true for our children. If their minds are filled with uplifting and positive messages, they will most likely feel uplifted and positive. If we have filled their bodies with good food, they are more likely to be healthy physically, and if they are fed with uplifting messages, they are more likely to be spiritually healthy. If we feed them junk food and a substandard diet, they have a greater possibility of falling prey to health issues and illness. If they are mentally consuming angry thoughts, negative messages, and violent images, they will be more inclined to develop an unhealthy mental state and weak spirituality. We need to be aware of the mental and emotional diet of our children. This is a tough task, but it is one we must take on. The images and concepts presented to our children through social media and easily accessed internet information are beyond the emotional readiness of children. We are allowing this input to damage the psychological and emotional condition of our children. This damage impedes the development of a healthy sense of self. Anxiety and emotional issues among children increase while parents remain disconnected and unaware of the intellectual intake of their children. We as parents are guilty of profound ignorance of this topic. Large numbers of parents are completely unaware of the information diet their children are consuming.

Do not be misled: "Bad company corrupts good character." (1 Corinthians 15:33 NIV)

As a teacher I have had many opportunities to talk with young people on this topic. So often they will say something along the lines of, "Well, it's not that bad." One of my responses: "If I am driving on a very long straight road and am only one degree away from steering straight on that road, at first no one would notice. But after a certain distance down the road, the one-degree angle will begin to generate a variance that will put the car off the road. What seems like a small thing, only a single degree off true center, becomes significant and eventually makes staying on the road impossible." I have encountered students who genuinely have a lack of understanding when it comes to discerning between right and wrong. The distorted input during the psychological developmental phases of their childhoods has caused an inability to generate a solid moral base. What once was unthinkable to a twelve-year-old child has become unclear to them as a result. I asked a class of students how important it is to get good grades. Of course they answered that it is very important. Then I asked them how much cheating they would do to get a good grade. The response was telling. Most of the students needed me to define what I would determine as cheating.

It is important that we stay true to course in the area of what goes into our children's minds. There are several components to this that deserve attention. We must be aware of the images and messages they consume through the vast array of media they access. The age of controlling what is seen on TV and feeling like the job is done is over. A diligent approach involves cybercontrols on home computers as well as mobile devices. Staying true to course also involves monitoring social media accounts and remaining current on the various trends within the variety of social media offerings. If you aren't current on what is happening with these sites, do some investigating. Use a simple google search, or ask other parents to get you caught up with the latest trends. Realize that in a few short weeks, there will be a new trend. This means you need to work to stay current. It is imperative that you know what is coming at your kids through the cyberworld and social media, which has grown into a significant part of teen socialization. A simple step of following all the same accounts your children follow will allow you to gain awareness of what they see daily and is a great way to start. Making certain your children do their group cybergame play in your presence is crucial. Your child should not "game" in a remote or private location without accountability regarding the persons they interact with or the length of time spent. This means sacrificing your screen time to be in the same place your child is gaming. It is shocking to listen to teens in my classroom discuss the hours spent and people met in this format. Additionally, the images and psychological impact are something a parent should monitor well beyond the industry rating on the game. This is another area where all the adults involved in your child's life must communicate and agree to the same approach no matter how they feel about each other. The good of your child must be the top priority.

A partner to the understanding of images and media influences is genuine knowledge of your children's friends. Make it easy for your children to have friends over at your home. Listen to the conversations, and learn from them. Know what is important to your child and your child's friends. Resist the temptation to indulge in nights of peace and quiet by sending your child over to a friend's house regularly. This will prevent you from staying connected with the friends who are an influence on your child. The opportunities for quiet evenings and lots of rest will come sooner than you think. Embrace the noise, and learn about who your child has as friends.

As well as embracing the noise, allow your children to be spontaneous and even slightly chaotic. One year when one of my children was in high school, the homecoming weekend involved an invitation to a party. The parents were going to be home. On the surface, it looked like a fun and safe situation. My child shared with me discussions of potential disruption. Some students planned to sneak alcohol in to the party. My child wanted to attend but also wanted to leave if that did happen. So I dropped a carload of high school kids off, parked my car a block away, and waited. It wasn't long before a message came to my phone to come and get my children. With them were several more students who also wanted to leave. One of them had the type of parents we should all strive to be. Those parents told me and another mom driver to bring the whole group to their house. A spur-of-the-moment party was thrown together. In the end, the students had a great time, and the parents who did not let the lack of planning and organization stop them had an opportunity to meet and get to know dozens of their child's friends. It would be great to have things planned and organized. The important point is, what wolf will you feed? The night of the impromptu party relocation, the parents who opened the doors of their home fed the good wolf a feast!

In addition to the opportunity to know the children whom their child calls friends, the parents who opened their home also provided a safe place and accessible options for their child and the other children involved, promoting and affirming making good choices. Starting when they are very young, you need to help your kids understand choices—the good results of wise, spirit-led decisions and the negative results of questionable motivations in choice making. Allow your children to practice choice making consistently as a part of most things. When children grow up with choices as a part of their daily thinking, they often understand the results of choices with ease. This is simple to do when your children are very young. I would pick out two different, yet acceptable clothing choices for my children and then offer them the choice of what to wear from those. Choosing a drink with dinner was done in the same manner: I would set out two acceptable choices and allow them to choose. This establishes the practice of making choices and provides opportunities for success when making good choices when they are learning the simple tasks of life as toddlers. Putting as many opportunities in front of them to make choices while setting them up to make a good choice is a great place to start building a foundation that will lead to a person who understands the gains of a good choice and the value of being decisive.

As children grow into the preteen years and you allow them to choose from all the options possible, be sure to clearly establish the results of a poor choice. When a poor choice is made, remove the opportunity to choose. For example, when my children were not limited to two choices for a drink with dinner and they chose a soda instead of a healthy drink, I told them that since they were not able to make a good choice, I would choose for them. It quickly became clear to them that they needed to think through the choices they made. It is far better for the poor choices and resulting consequences to happen in the preteen years when the consequence is water with dinner and a lack of options than to have them make poor choices when they are older and the consequence is significant disciplinary action. Consistently offering and responding to choices is simple: "Choose a drink for dinner." "I want a soda." "You clearly aren't going to make a good choice on this, so I will choose for you"—and then choose a least favorite drink. When they complain and ask for an acceptable alternative, say *no*. Tell them they can choose that tomorrow. It is better for them to learn from one less favorite drink at dinner than from a huge, costly consequence later in life.

As they become teens, be prepared to discuss choices and help generate solutions to prevent the choosing of an undesirable option. This will take honesty and a willingness to predict outcomes. While it is not easy, you will need to be supportive of the decisions your children make and trust them. The time when this was most challenging for me was my son's first year of high school. It involved trusting a decision he had made. He attended tryouts for a school team and, after only a few sessions, came home and told me he would not play for the team regardless of how the tryouts went. I couldn't understand his choice, but I trusted him. In time it became clear to me that he had made a good choice as the coach was dismissed, and the team my son had chosen to work out with generated significant gains for him in his sport. I am so thankful I had a history of teaching him to choose and trusted his choice.

As you work to make sure your children are making good choices and are focused on uplifting and positive images and messages, you also need to be certain you are giving them positive input. How we respond to their performance and work ethic is a significant part of this. Too often we get caught up in the emphasis of the present moment, be it the score of the game or the standing of the team in the rankings. We can lose sight of the important life lessons that events are teaching our children and fill them with negative self-perceptions and destructive messages. I have been as guilty as any parent of being extremely proud of my children when they garner the highest score in the class on a test or score the winning goal. Those are momentary achievements. What I need to emphasize to my children is the work ethic and the total effort that went into the preparation for that moment. Through my years of teaching I have seen so many examples of the student who was not a standout in middle school or even high school but who went on to accomplish great things. My children went to the same middle school as a young man who eventually played football in the NFL. While he was in middle school he was an average football player. However, he was blessed with parents who taught him to work hard and to believe in himself and in the process he was working through. We need to make sure that we are not feeding the minds of our children messages that emphasize winning over work ethic. We need to be certain that we celebrate effort and faith, and support honesty and integrity. These messages will ring in our children's hearts and minds for years after we have delivered them, so we must make certain they are messages that promote the characteristics leading to strong faith and an emotionally healthy adult.

When you are supporting and cheering for your child, keep perspective. Ask yourself if you can remember doing things at the age your child is currently and how pivotal it was in hindsight. We have all heard the ranting parent who wants to see the win at the soccer game of eight-year-olds. We have all heard the bragging parent at the student award assembly because his or her child won first place in the second-grade science fair. We need to understand the misplaced priorities resulting from this adult behavior. Children learn to value the outcome, to value the win, over integrity or hard work. That is not a value system supporting an adult who is emotionally healthy or genuinely successful.

When I was in grade school I was helping my dad do some yard work one afternoon. I don't remember exactly what work we were doing or what I had done to earn the moment that happened. At one point my dad looked up from his work and said, "I knew I could count on you to get this done. You are not afraid of hard work"—one simple statement that still makes me feel like a champion forty years later. I have faced a lot of challenges and difficulties while raising two children as a widowed mom. Every time it has seemed overwhelming, I hear my dad say, "You are not afraid of hard work." That statement has carried me through some long days of some genuinely hard work. I pray I have seized the moments and opportunities to speak statements like that to my children. I pray they will know how much I admire their fortitude, integrity, work ethic, and faith. Mostly, I pray I have fed those types of messages to my children to keep their mental and emotional nourishment healthy.

We know there are plenty of times when we will need to present negative feedback to our children. This is another source of mental feeding we need to attend to carefully. How we present negative information when they need to hear it is very important. We need to make certain we are presenting constructive direction and not just the "what you did wrong" message. This is a skill many teachers learn quickly. If you want a classroom full of children not to talk to each other, the most ineffective thing to say is, "Don't talk." The effective approach is to give them instruction on what they should be doing and how. Instructions such as "Silently begin writing the paragraph" focus their minds on the task to be done, not the undesirable action. If you are working to correct and redirect your child, focus the feedback on the desired outcome.

When my daughter was young, she was reluctant to join in with children in new settings. She would want to hang on to my leg or at least my hand and stay back. If I pushed her forward, it only added more anxiety. I found that if I could locate one child she already knew or a toy in the room I knew she enjoyed playing with and then point out to her that her friend or the toy was just a few feet away, she would go to it easily. Soon she would be joining in with the other children happily. We need to purposefully point our children in the direction we want them to pursue, not just provide negative feedback about the direction they have already traveled. Just as our affirmations of work ethic and character will stay with them for years, a harmful negative statement will do the same. Be prayerful as you correct your children. They need correction and they need redirection, but they do not need a parent who adds more negative thoughts to what is already coming at them every day.

In Exodus chapter 17 we read of the Amalekites. They have shown up to attack the Israelites as they are making their way through the desert. They attack the Israelites, and the Israelites spend an entire day fighting back. This could possibly be like a regular day for someone trying to walk closely with God today. Messages, images, confused priorities, all come at us and our children; we are the target of the attack. Our progress is hindered, and we are distracted and often defeated. We enjoy an abundance of blessings from God. We need to work to keep our children aware of all that is good and from God. We need to make sure they are thinking on those things and not the things the "Amalekites" would show them. Today's world has an abundance of "Amalekites" who will seek to distract and defeat you. If you make anything more important to you than your relationship with God or more important than God's plan, God's will, or God's claim on your life, then that thing becomes an "Amalekite." The negative messages and distracting images that flood the screens in front of our children's faces have the potential to pull them so far off the course of God's will that we have no choice but to see these things as an attack. We also can't make the mistake taught to us in 1 Samuel chapter 15. King Saul was told to eliminate the Amalekites, but he did not follow God's leading. He kept that which he deemed to be good and only eliminated what he felt was weak or unappealing. He compromised instead of following what God had led him to do. I know as a parent, I have struggled to always maintain the true course. We compromise so our children can fit in or gain approval from others. Then we want to make sure they don't compromise. The "Amalekites" are all around us. We need to be vigilant as we raise our children. We must model for them an uncompromising approach to our focus on God and all the good God provides. If we are willing to pick out the things we deem good and eliminate only the things we perceive as distasteful, then we will demonstrate compromise to our children. We need to do all we can to keep them focused on God, the goodness of God, and all of God's blessings.

As a parent who has watched one child grow into an adult with another close behind, I can assure you that the efforts to keep the messages and images focused on whatever is good, true, noble, right, pure, lovely, admirable, and praiseworthy have been worth all the energy involved. The "Amalekites" still attacked, and the negative influences distracted the focus. Just like in the legend of the wolves, the fight still occurs. Thankfully, prior to the fight, there was a concerted effort to feed the good wolf, and the good wolf won.

WORTHY OF PRAISE

———◇———

Great is the Lord, and most worthy of praise, in the city
of our God, his holy mountain

—Psalm 48:1 (NIV)

One of my favorite television shows is the classic *Andy Griffith Show*. The life of those living in Mayberry seems ideal and so simple. There is very little that causes confusion or uncertainty. Every Sunday everyone attends church and has Sunday supper as a family. Church is the center of the community. Everything seems right in Mayberry. Is it possible the priorities of family and worship portrayed in the show are the strong foundations we seem to be letting fall apart in our modern culture? We need to build on this foundation of worship and praise of God. To establish a family grounded in the practice of praising God—of praising what is worthy of praise—is to put one's family on the course of genuine sacred joy. As a parent, it is my job to determine what foundation my home rests on.

Building a solid foundation starts with laying the cornerstone of regular worship attendance. Too often we act as though worship is negotiable. It is not. We need to be there, and churches are making it easier than ever to be there. Worship styles vary, and almost any style of worship can be accessed. Additionally, most churches are offering Saturday evening options as well as Sunday morning services. With all of the variety and time options, you can find something that meets the needs and preferences of your family. Don't be stuck on worshipping in the style you prefer most. Find what speaks to your children and makes them excited about going to church, and go.

I once heard a pastor tell a story about those who felt they did not need to be in church to maintain their faith walk. A pastor was visiting a man who did not want to attend church. Instead of talking to him about the topic, he sat quietly with him and watched the fire burning in the fireplace. Then he used the fire tongs, took a hot ember from the fire, and placed it on the hearth. Away from the fire the ember slowly cooled and became colorless and dark. A few more moments of silence passed, and the pastor picked up the ember and tossed it back into the fire, where it gained heat and began to glow again. This is a fantastic representation of the value of church attendance for those who are seeking to walk in faith.

Worship is a means to praise God and maintain our focus on what is truly worthy of praise. It is a place where we commune with God and grow in our relationship with God, and where we gain strength from those around us who are seeking to do the same. Another important aspect of worship and praise is the way it protects our emotional and psychological state. It is hard to remain defeated or sorrow-filled when singing praises to God. Praising God fills our minds with reflections of God's goodness and moves the negative images and thoughts of this world out. If we allow the negativity of life in this world to take hold of our thoughts and feelings, we will suffer and struggle consistently. We have one sure way to prevent that from happening: praise.

I have a close friend who is also a widowed mom. Her philosophy is to have her children at church every time the doors are open. If the activity isn't inclusive of youth, they will volunteer in the nursery. She simply keeps them involved in their church. Her daughters have grown into lovely God-centered women. Clearly her philosophy has worked well for them. For that family, church is as much a part of life as school, work, and dinnertime.

Regular participation in the life of the church and regular attendance in worship provides a foundation for and depth to the family history that your children will need later in life. We need to demonstrate our faithful attendance in worship, our faithful participation in the life of the church, and our faith response as those who tithe, and we need to experience the intimate act of worship as a family. When your children can answer the questions "What is your parent's favorite hymn?" and "What is your parent's favorite scripture?", then you are on the right track. We as parents also need to recognize that our children will have a desire to establish their own worship styles and tastes. We need to know what our kids' worship style is and what their favorite worship songs, scriptures, and Bible stories are. There is a depth of family history in these moments of worship that will carry our children through the tough times when we are not present.

When our kids watch us worship, and when they worship with us, then worship becomes a part of their understanding of home. We can provide through regular worship an intertwined experience of family and home involving God as the head of the family and being the core definition of home and family. This regular experience becomes as much a part of their family experience and definition as family meals, evening prayer, conversation in the car, chores, and all the traditions and functions of family life. When they long for home, hopefully they will recall the foundation we have laid of faithful worship leading them to God and to worship.

As my daughter went through college, she would come home for holidays. The most important aspect of her time at home was our going to church together. She would be extremely disappointed if a favorite song was not sung or a traditional aspect of the service had been changed. She genuinely connected her worship memories to a sense of home. The Christmas Eve service when the soloist changed his approach to "O Holy Night" and sang it very differently from what she had heard growing up was not a happy one for her. To be perfectly honest, it was an extremely happy Christmas Eve for me. While she was disappointed, I was thrilled to learn that worship was so significant to her concept of home. Worship is where your children will learn to value the relationship they have with God. As you strive to keep the Sabbath and make it a family priority, your children will learn to value what is genuinely worthy of praise.

We must be aware that what is valued by the world is often not consistent with our faith or who we are called to be as disciples of Christ. Consistent regular attendance in worship nurtures spiritual growth and the growth of our relationship with God, enabling us to view things from God's perspective.

We are constantly tempted to define faith by worldly conditions. If we are successful by worldly standards, then clearly we are faithful and our relationship with God is good. This is a thought process that is not theologically sound, and it is not one that will remain stable when the challenges of life come. We like this type of thinking when things are going our way. We like to think the approach we are using is fine if we are getting good results. Regular worship and focus on spiritual growth will refute this thinking. Human reasoning can cause us to justify the means by gauging the results. It is tempting to focus on getting applause and not focus on the consistent worship and praise of God. As we maintain regular worship, we guide our children to a place where the relationship with God becomes the focus, not the results applauded by those around them. Worship is the place we can teach our children to think from a God-centered perspective. They come to realize that it is not what you do but *how* you do what you do that matters. God does not think like human beings think, and God does not value what human beings value.

Unfortunately our current culture values a victory over integrity. We must teach our children to value what God values. Christ sets the example for us of a servant's heart and teaches us that the first will be last and the last will be first. We need to guide our children to develop a deep relationship with God to keep these understandings at the forefront of their thinking. Regular worship and focus on what is genuinely worthy of praise will help. Through worship, we stay focused on Christ. The Christ example should be our focus and goal.

> See to it that no one takes you captive through hollow and deceptive philosophy, which depends on human tradition and the elemental spiritual forces of this world rather than on Christ. (Colossians 2:8 NIV)

Scripture tells us in several places and in several ways that God judges the heart of a person. If our hearts are focused on our relationship with God, our hearts will be in the right place and all other things will fall into place. This doesn't mean we will be rich and successful. It means the genuine sacred joy that will fill our lives will generate a true sense of contentment in all circumstances. We live in a world where awards, titles, prestige, and a win–loss column seem to dominate our thinking.

Honestly, it seems like a "win at all costs" and "the end justifies the means" attitude is dominant. Our children see this. Our children are exposed to this. Participation awards and false praise are not the answer. We can't pretend our children have met the worldly standard for awards and the right number of wins to look good to others and hope also to teach them to value the heart of what they do. The participation award is actually counterproductive. Participation awards say to our children that the award is the important factor. We need to teach our children that even if the number in the loss column is bigger, the important part is the work ethic, effort, honorable approach, and the way they glorify God in how they do what they do.

Life involves losses. Our children will face days when they feel they lost or when the score shows them they lost. Our job as parents is not to sugarcoat and disguise a loss, but to build the character in our children so that they may see beyond a loss to the depth of effort. Even more important is to build people who seek to glorify God in how they work to become who God has created them to be. As a parent, I have watched my children play more games than I can count. I have cheered through softball games, basketball games, flag football games, baseball games, soccer games, full-contact football games, cross-country meets, and track meets. Some of those competitions were wins, and others were not. I honestly can't tell you how many times my children won or lost. What I do know is they learned more from the losses than they ever did from the wins. I can also honestly tell you that the moments I recall as my most treasured mom moments have nothing to do with the score. They are moments when the Christ in my children showed through to those watching, moments such as the time when a player from the opposing team was injured and my son was the first to stop and check on the player and then stay with him, offering comfort, until his coach got to them. There is the memory of the night my daughter was prepared for an important AP test in high school, but stayed up and helped a friend study until she felt equally as prepared. These represent the moments that stand out in my memory. The time I heard my son say to his team, "Let's pray before the game" is another treasured memory. When my son's high school soccer team gathered to pray for an injured player on the opposing team and invited the opposing team to join them, or when they gathered to pray together after they lost the playoff game—these stand out as highlight moments in my memory. I have watched both of my children encourage teammates who were struggling and have seen them congratulate teammates who have garnered accolades. My daughter was so supportive of the star runner on the cross-country team that the coach invited my daughter to travel to the Regional Championship meet to support that runner. I also experienced great mom moments when after a cross-country season, my daughter wanted to do something special to thank her coach, and when after a game, my son remembered to thank his coaches for the time they give him, and he also thanked me for the support I gave him.

As cheering parents, we have a tendency to get caught up in the thrill of victory, but we must remember that in the long term, what we need our children to learn is that it's not what they do but *how* they do what they do that will honor their relationship with God. Seeking this relationship, and honoring it through their actions every day, is what needs to be the priority. The foregoing examples given are mostly in athletics, but the principle of making sure our children learn to value the way they go about living applies to all aspects of life. We must be diligent in teaching our children to praise what is genuinely worthy of praise, and not what the world deems worthy.

Seeing your child win the contest is fun—but you must keep your parent pride in check and look for, find, and praise the times in that contest when your child demonstrated Christ to all those watching. The times when our children act with integrity or with mercy and grace must be the victory we are cheering for. We must condition ourselves to watch for the moments when our children show others the love of Christ, and we must praise these moments. We need to strive to teach our children to value Christ like character more than victory. This doesn't mean they can't be fierce competitors. They should still seek to maximize the use of the gifts and blessings they receive from God. We must teach them to be fierce competitors only to the point where their witness is not compromised and the *how* they do what they do is pleasing to God. It is our task to watch the consistency of the witness more than we watch the scoreboard, the class rank and GPA, the judge's ratings, or the volume of the crowd's applause.

We are to love God with all our hearts, souls, minds, and strength. This does not show up in stats and rankings. It shows as the heart is revealed through words and actions. We need to be purposeful in praising and lifting up that which grows a beautiful heart. In doing that, we also need to be intentional about keeping worldly accomplishment and praise in perspective. We have to do this not just with our children but also with our own thinking. We also seek the approval of the world and seek to fill up our win column in our own ways. We need the break from the rush and push that is our daily life more than we realize. Taking time in worship to center our thinking on the how of all we do is vitally important. We need to be aware that our children learn from our actions far more than from our words.

It is never wise to define God's work in human terms. Further, it is not wise to define success by human accolades. We are given an example of this in the book of Matthew, chapter 19, when the rich young ruler approaches Jesus and asks what things he must do to achieve eternal life. He wants an action list to generate an accomplishment. This is the way we function in our human condition. We all understand the approach of listing the needed steps to accomplish the end goal. Jesus does not give the young ruler the answer he is seeking. In fact, the answer Jesus gives him is ultimately defeating for the wealthy man. Many read this scripture and think it is about wealth, but what Jesus is asking of the young man is about his heart and the priorities in his heart, not his net worth. The young ruler is seeking an achievement he can accomplish through earthly standards. What Jesus offers him is not a list of things to accomplish but rather a complete change of heart. That change of heart is what we are to be teaching our children. We must recognize that all the lists, accomplishments, awards, and honors are not going to put our children in the position to achieve genuine sacred joy in life. What will allow them to achieve sacred joy is a heart that seeks to please God and to value what God values. The best place for our children to learn what God values is in worship and in the various faith-growth opportunities found at church.

The rich young ruler pursued God intellectually but not by experience. What experiences are you willing to have? What adjustments are you willing to make to respond positively to Christ and experience the abundant joy of a relationship with him today? How will you model the experience-based relationship with God for your children? We need time in worship as much as our children do, not just for ourselves and our relationship with God, but also to strengthen our modeling to our children. This is what will keep our hearts in relationship with God and our praise focused on what is genuinely worthy of praise.

Choosing to worship God, praise what is worthy, and obey Christ, we will gain the opportunity to make a difference for ourselves and our children. We may not be able to go back in time to Mayberry, but we can lay a foundation for our children of worship, teach them to praise that which is worthy of praise, and experience sacred joy.

Accept Your Weaknesses—Ask for Help

---◇---

"Not by might nor by power, but by my Spirit," says the Lord Almighty.

—Zechariah 4:6 (NIV)

In the Old Testament we read the history of the nation of Israel. We read of the history involving the formation of Israel, the kings, and the struggles. When we read about the years of exile, we learn about the people of Israel exiled in Babylon for seventy years. When the Israelites finally returned to Jerusalem, they found the temple destroyed and the city in ruins. Now they faced rebuilding city walls as well as an entire city and a temple with no resources.

I know that as a single parent, I have often connected with this point in the history of the nation of Israel. I imagine many single parents can relate to this. We feel exiled in so many ways. We feel the need to rebuild our families and our lives, but we lack the knowledge and the resources. Our situation seems impossible. We need to remember that all the resources of heaven are at our disposal. I must also remember that not by my power or by my might will I rebuild my family, but by the power of the Spirit. I don't have to be strong enough or smart enough or wise enough to rebuild my family on my own. God is strong enough, with wisdom beyond my thinking, and will guide me. I don't have to have an abundance of resources; God will provide what my family needs. I don't need to fear that I will be rebuilding alone; God is with me, and I am not alone in this.

Just like the people of Israel, we are hurt and damaged. In fact at many points we feel a bit like we are in exile. God wanted to restore Israel, and God wants to heal your wounds. If we refuse to admit that we have faults and struggles, then we can't expect the healing touch of God. We are all in need of God's healing touch, and we all have wounds that desperately need healing. If you hide your wounds, they cannot receive the healing touch they need. Accept your weaknesses and faults without fear. When your wounds, weakness, and faults are exposed, God will be reaching out to heal them. Exposing our needs is hard to do, yet it is worth the struggle. Our culture does not embrace weakness, and our children need our strength. Those two issues combine to put us in a difficult place when it comes to accepting our limitations and weaknesses. We don't want to let our children down, because we know they have been through so much already. We see those perfectly filtered happy images on social media telling us how happy everyone else is. So when we feel down and we are struggling, we wonder if there is any place where our weakness is not unacceptable. The good news is this: there is! In our weakness, God's strength is on display, and God is glorified as he is seen by others as our strength. We don't have to be perfection in a social media picture. We are perfection in the eyes of God, and we are able to accomplish amazing things through the strength he provides.

The easiest way to access the strength God offers is to acknowledge our weaknesses and place them in the hands of God. I have learned over the years that my weaknesses are ranked. There are a few at the top of the list that generate greater struggles than those further down the list. I think loneliness is at the top of my list of weaknesses. I probably waste the more time and have the biggest pity parties because of loneliness. The ironic part of this is that God is with me all the time. I am never alone. Despite this truth, I do miss the sense of being known by someone that people in a healthy marriage experience. My late husband really understood me, and I genuinely understood him. The ability to share thoughts, have discussions, and be authentic while knowing I was loved at the same time was a treasure. I miss being known and loved despite my flaws. I believe this is the source of my struggle with loneliness. Like I stated, I have wasted time and energy on pity parties and have made pointless attempts to make myself busy enough so as not to feel the sting of the loneliness. In the end, the only solution to my problem was to completely give my loneliness to God.

We hear "give it to God" all the time, but what does that really mean? For me, that meant taking steps to involve my spiritual growth and prayer time in this area. To deal with the pity party habit, I started keeping a daily praise journal. Every day I would write down one simple thing I was grateful for. The act of focusing on what was a blessing each day generated a shift in my thinking. When I would start to slip back into self-pity, I would look back over my journal and all the small and large blessings that fill my days. Additionally, I earnestly prayed for God to change my heart in regard to the loneliness I felt. Every day I would ask for a change, and over time, my heart has changed. I still long for someone to know me, but first, I want to know and love my children well. My heart longs to nurture the relationship I have with them, to allow them to feel authentic and genuine in the communications and responses we share. Most importantly, I long to allow them to feel completely known and loved by me. A parent–child relationship like that takes effort and energy and will be a blessing for me and for my children for the rest of our lives. I don't want to miss one possible moment with them when I can be hearing about their day or listening to the concerns on their hearts. All of this has come as a result of constant prayer, seeking God's hand in healing my shattered heart. I don't have someone who knows me and loves me here on earth, but I have a God who knows me very well, even the number of hairs on my head, right down to how many of them would be gray if it weren't for the hair dye, and loves me anyway. My consistent prayer, lifting my greatest weakness to God, has allowed God to heal my heart and change it. I treasure the time I have with my children, and I know by faith that when they are grown and have moved out of my house, God will fill my life with daily blessings and provide a focus for my heart that will continue to crowd out any room for loneliness. This is how I gave my weakness to God. It is how any of us, after identifying our weaknesses, can let God heal us and transform us.

I am not saying I never feel loneliness. I still feel it. It hits at the most unpredictable times, and then also at the predictable times. The predictable times require what I have come to call an exit strategy or escape plan. An example of the "exit strategy" idea is the time I had to attend a banquet for my son, shortly after my daughter had spread her adult wings and moved away. I knew I was in a tender place emotionally, so I planned carefully. I set up a time for coffee right after the banquet with a friend. I knew going home after the banquet would be emotionally difficult, and since my son had just gained a driver's license and would be driving his date, I would be driving to the venue and back home alone. Both my children living their independence and an event of reflecting and celebrating achievements was the perfect mixture for a struggle, and I knew it. So I set an exit strategy in place: coffee with a friend and time to catch up and have her tell me about the recent activities in her life.

When we accept our weaknesses, we can also recognize when we need to plan or prepare for moments that might be a potential struggle. Sometimes they rise up at the most unpredictable times and blindside us, and those times call for fervent prayer and personal acceptance of ourselves and our weaknesses. When we can plan, we should have an exit strategy in place. That is one of the benefits of allowing ourselves to see our weaknesses and come to peace with them as a source through which God's healing and power may shine.

I wish I only had the weakness of loneliness to deal with. The truth is, I have a storehouse of weaknesses. I struggle with a lot of different aspects of my humanness. If we are honest, we can all say the same. In each area of weakness, we need to be willing to allow God to be our strength and to provide for us what we need. Another one of my areas of weakness is self-doubt. I feel this most when I have to make big decisions and immediately begin questioning the decision I made. It is times like this that I need to trust the people God has placed in my life and ask them for feedback or input. I also need to spend time in prayer and seek the peace that God can use to guide me. When I am faced with the feeling of fatigue and overload, I confront my weakness of denial. I need to accept I am limited in my energy and abilities. I also need to accept that I may not have a perfectly clean home or everything checked off on my to-do list at the end of each day. I also need to accept the fact that others are more equipped to handle some of the things overwhelming me and that God has put them in my life to be helpful to me and to my children. Accepting my weaknesses allows me to accept help from those who bless me with help when I am overloaded. Our points of weakness simply require asking for help from those God has placed in our lives to help us!

I have gotten good at eating alone in restaurants, going to parties and weddings without a plus-one, and doing all the somewhat predictable stuff. I haven't gotten good at reading my daughter's latest magazine publication or watching my son score a goal alone—those still hurt. The times when my child does something amazing and I realize I am standing there alone still make me feel weak. The moments when I accomplish something and there is no one to tell are challenging. I felt so much weakness when I received recognition for my twenty-fifth anniversary at work. It was a hard and lonely day for me. Even on those types of days, I can teach my children something very valuable. I can show them we all have weaknesses, and we all have struggles, and the healthiest way to deal with those is to go through them, not avoid them. We can embrace the people God places in our lives to help us go through these moments of weakness and struggle. These moments allow our children to learn through our modeling that weaknesses are not something to hide or things that should cause shame. God will place the most unusual and wonderful things in our lives to help us.

When my son was about nine, he became keenly aware of the lack of a dad in the house, particularly at night. He wanted to be able to protect the house, but he was only a boy. He struggled with this, and I felt intense weakness because I could not find a way to help him. No amount of talking, locking doors, leaving lights on, or providing assurances would help. I prayed for a way to give him a sense of security, but I could not generate it. Then, a friend called me to let me know she had a rescue dog that needed a home. She felt this dog needed my son. I did not want a puppy at the time. Reluctantly I agreed to let the dog come over to the house and meet the family. That dog never left. What is miraculous was that the dog was the answer to my son's struggle. He slept in my son's room and was a constant companion for him. Because the dog was half Great Dane, he grew into a big dog very quickly. Also, because he was big, my son felt we were all well protected. The truth is that our sweet dog would not do a lot to protect our house at all. But that did not matter. The miracle was that my son felt secure and believed he had the needed resource in his dog to protect his family. God has solutions for all the moments when we don't have answers, or strength, or knowledge. We must go to God in prayer and then step into situations by faith, understanding that God is glorified when our weaknesses magnify his strength. This is just one of the times I have watched God provide. What we need as single parents is not perfection. We need the ability to ask for help and then accept help when God provides.

After a lot of years of parenting alone I have learned to ask for help as soon as I feel the need. I have a dear friend who is a wonderful prayer warrior. I call her or message her as soon as I know I am in a place of need. She will immediately pray for me and for the situation. I have also learned to listen to her when she feels she has an answer to those prayers. God has provided many solutions and helped us through many struggles with her as a part of his strength in my weaknesses. As I have learned from her, I have also learned from others who have stepped in to help solve issues for us. I have learned to ask for advice instead of wanting to hide the fact that I don't know answers. I have learned to ask for help with home and auto repairs instead of trying to do everything myself while pretending that I am perfectly capable of making any repair or doing any maintenance project. I have learned to ask for help with the things my children need, like teaching my daughter to ride a horse or teaching my son how to hit a baseball. When I don't try to pretend that I am without weakness, God sends the perfect people into our lives to help with each situation.

Most importantly I have learned to accept help without casting judgment on myself for needing help. Too often we judge ourselves as weak or needy for allowing others to help us. We are so willing to help but not as willing to be helped. We need to accept our weaknesses without judging ourselves, and we need to allow those around us to step up and help us. We need to remove the expectation of perfection to allow God to work in all the many ways he can. God may be using our weakness and need for help as a means to show someone around us the gift he has given them. As we allow these people to help us, they can discover a purpose God may have for them in our area of weakness. Our accepting our weaknesses may be a piece of God's plan for another person's life. We don't need to be perfect. What we need is the ability to ask for help and accept help when it is offered.

We don't help our children by hiding our weaknesses or pretending we don't make mistakes. We give our children the opportunity to know we understand they will make mistakes because we make mistakes. We need to model that we know mistakes happen by admitting our own. We give our children the opportunity to experience both sides of grace by admitting our errors and allowing our children to offer us grace in those situations. I will never forget the day I got the times of one of my son's soccer games wrong. We arrived at the game at the time I thought it was scheduled, only to find that the game was already half over. I was so upset with myself for ruining my son's game day. After the game was over, I apologized to him and the coach over and over again. My son simply said, "It's OK, Mom." He wasn't angry or anything. He gave me grace. In that moment, he learned through experience what "forgive us as we forgive those who have trespassed against us" is all about. He lived forgiving and became stronger in his ability to forgive because I was willing to admit my weakness that day.

Accepting my weakness demonstrates for my children many valuable lessons that are much better taught through modeling than through words. I get the chance to show them true humility. It instills the type of humility that will help them recognize that regardless of accomplishments or achievements, we are all precious and loved by God. I also demonstrate through priceless experiences that God does show up every time we have a need. When children know our weaknesses and see God provide, faith is built by experience that goes heart deep for them.

My children were very aware of my inability to cook. After I was widowed, a wonderful chef from my church began preparing meals for us and leaving them in my freezer. All I had to do was warm them up each evening. My children lived a life filled with God providing our daily bread literally. And when God provides what they know we are not capable of providing for ourselves, gratitude grows naturally in their hearts. Gratitude will prevent them from feeling prideful or entitled because they know God is blessing them beyond what they or I could have earned for them. Allowing one's needs to be met by accepting help is beneficial to more than just a parent with a weakness.

Possibly one of the greatest benefits of accepting your weakness is that you will teach your children to recognize their own limitations and do so without self-condemnation. Our culture has created a very unrealistic "everyone is a winner" approach with children. The fact is that all of us, adults and children, have limitations and weaknesses. I certainly would not be a winner in a cooking contest! If we can accept our weaknesses and defeats without self-condemnation, and if we teach our children by example how to do so as well, we will teach a very valuable life skill that will serve our children well in the future.

I say all of this with a warning. When accepting our weaknesses, we need to be cautious not to share too much with children. Some things are not age-appropriate or emotionally healthy for our children. There is great value in a trusted friend or family member to confide in about the bigger and more complicated weaknesses. As children get older and are better able to process various complicated topics, you can decide then if they should hear about your more significant weaknesses.

My daughter was very concerned about my loneliness, so much so that she found it very important for me to date. I think I should have worked harder at not allowing her to be as aware of my loneliness as she was. We all have to work to keep such revelation and privacy in a healthy balance. Our children need us to be honest with them, and we need to accept we have weaknesses and allow them to see our weaknesses. Balance is needed, though. We do not want to make them into miniature adults who take on the role of confidant or caretaker for us. We are the adults, and they are children.

As for the question of dating and remarrying and how that should be handled, prayer is the only right answer. God has a plan for each of us and is working to give us his best and to give our children his best. We need to seek God's will and trust the outcome of following his will, confident that his will can produce abundant joy! As I look back over the years I have been raising my children as a single parent, I feel I wasted valuable time I could have spent with my children by trying to pursue dating relationships. Additionally, although I tried not to introduce gentlemen I dated to my children, they still met some, and I am not confident the influence of those men added anything of value to their lives. On the contrary, there were some influences introduced to my children I feel were mostly negative in the final outcome. I honestly regret spending time trying to date while I was raising my children. Now as the time of having my children in my house is coming to an end, I deeply wish I had embraced every possible moment with my children and not allowed the distraction and negative input of dating. I am not saying that this is going to be the same for every single parent. I think we need to earnestly seek God and his will for our lives. If God is leading a single parent to a healthy, God-centered dating relationship, then that relationship will bring more good into the lives of that parent and the children involved than they would have experienced without that relationship. There is not a "one size fits all" perfect answer to this question, except to pray and listen. Once you have discerned the will of God, accept it and follow it, and trust God for the outcome.

We need to accept that we desire relationship. It is the way we were created. Humans are relational beings. God created us to be in relationship with him. In Genesis we read of God creating the universe and all that we experience. God made Adam and was in the garden with him in perfect union and relationship with him. Adam had everything he needed, and he had a perfect relationship with God. Yet God looked at Adam and could see he was alone and needed a partner. Here was Adam, a person who was in perfect relationship with God and still needed a partner. Isn't it understandable that we also desire a partner? Don't think this means you have to rush out and find a new spouse—you don't! In many cases, a quick, poor choice of a spouse is the last thing you or your children need. What you really need is to pray for guidance and to accept that God knows your needs and will supply them. What you need most is the ability to ask for help and accept help when it is offered. Accept help from others. If you can't accept help and will only offer help, you are passing judgment on those who need help. You are trying to pretend you are above needing help. Accept your weaknesses, and accept you do indeed need help.

When your weaknesses lead you to make mistakes, forgive yourself as readily as you forgive your children. Forgiveness is a powerful tool and a vital means of self-care. We need to push ourselves to forgive those who have hurt us and failed us. Forgiveness is the remedy for anger and bitterness. Bitterness will consume you from the inside and rob you of joy and happiness. Forgiving is not for the one forgiven but for the one who is doing the forgiving. Bitterness will destroy you. We must allow

God to remove the bitterness and replace it with grace. God's grace is sufficient to remove your bitterness and empower you to demonstrate forgiveness for your children. Just like becoming willing to forgive our children and seek forgiveness for our weaknesses, we need to find a way to forgive ourselves when we know we have hurt those we love, and we need to forgive those who hurt us. This models grace for our children and brings it to a heart level that enables them to truly accept the grace of the cross. It is not just a means of emotionally healthy living; it is also a means of a healthy faith walk for our children. The modeling of forgiveness puts our children into the practice of accepting God's grace and forgiveness of them.

Grace is sufficient for salvation, but it is also just as much a model for how we are to live, demonstrating and offering grace to those around us. We need to pass on the grace Christ has given us. We also need to enable our children to accept God's grace and demonstrate how they are to do this. We often forget that our ability to accept grace and forgiveness will teach our children how to accept it for themselves. We need to accept grace as readily as we give love, serve others, and demonstrate grace.

Jesus did not say that we would be known as Christians because of the way we recite scripture, or because of our flawless adherence to a strict moral code, or because of our ability to condemn those who fail to live up to our moral standard. In John 13:35 we are clearly told that the love we show to each other will demonstrate to the world our faith in Christ. They will know we are Christians by our love. We need to be able to accept love as well as we give it. Many are wonderful at giving but not as wonderful at accepting because an inability to accept and understand their own weaknesses and need for God's love, grace, and healing stands in the way. Knowing God loved us before we loved him and that he sacrificed his Son to atone for our wrongdoing should help us keep perspective on this. We forgive, and we need forgiveness. We need to accept our weaknesses and our need for forgiveness, and allow God to provide the help we need in the form of those he places in our lives to help us. We need to embrace the role we enjoy as children of God, forgiven and provided for. We give our children an invaluable gift when we teach them through our own lives that our identity is "child of God." We are more than our circumstances. We are not victims, and we are not perfect people. Rather, we are children of God. That is the identity we want to pass on to our children, and so that is what we need to live and demonstrate to them. We need to model the joy that comes from embracing the forgiveness and grace God provides, not a striving for perfection that only leads to disappointment and impossible expectations.

The only way we can avoid disappointment is to remain centered in our identity as children of God and to count on God to provide all we need. In the book of Joshua we learn of Joshua's promotion to leadership among the Israelites. He is called to fill the shoes of Moses and take the people into the Promised Land. They face armies that cause deep fear in their hearts. But they have a history demonstrating there is nothing to fear. God had defeated their enemies in the past and provided for their every need. Often when we are going through rough times, we are inclined to question if God is going to show up for us. We need to focus on the perspective of our history. We should be able to have the confidence of Joshua, knowing that God has kept his promises and provided for us.

> None of the good promises the Lord your God made to
> you has failed. Everything was fulfilled for you: not one
> promise has failed. (Joshua 23:14 NIV)

Scripture assures us that strife and struggle are not ours alone. We know our struggle is not the first one God has encountered. We need to trust that God will provide and that God can take our weaknesses and replace them with his strength. Scripture is full of stories of human weakness and God fulfilling promises. God promised Abraham and Sarah descendants, but it took twenty-five years for them to be able to see this promise fulfilled. There were twenty-four years of struggle and waiting. David received the anointing as the future king but found himself running for his life instead of sitting on a throne. Eventually he would look back on his long reign knowing that God had fulfilled his promises.

For us, we need to keep a record. Literally journal the moments you see the hand of God reaching out to you. Make notes of the times when

God provides your needs, where God fulfills a promise. This way, as you face the moments of struggle, you have perspective and knowledge that God will deliver on the promises you are holding in your heart. Your journal will remind you that God doesn't forget us and that God doesn't show up late. Keeping a record prevents us from feeling that we have to be perfect or that we have to generate the solution to every struggle. Keeping a journal helps us know we can count on God to be our strength.

> The Lord is not slow in keeping his promise as some understand slowness. Instead he is patient with you, not wanting anyone to perish, but everyone to come to repentance. (2 Peter 3:9 NIV)

Keep a journal so you can reflect on the works God has completed and have peace as you move through the hard times. Just know you will face really hard days. I have had days when I actually resorted to crying, ranting, and yelling at God when I was alone in my car. There are countless numbers of single parents who will admit to days like this. Go ahead and yell, rant, and cry. I assure you, God is big enough to handle your outburst. Just don't indulge in asking for an easy way out or a way to sidestep the real emotion. The fact is that parenting is most often thankless until your own children are parents. Then they will look at you and see you as a genius. In the time between now and that point, all you can do is be the best you possible. You won't be the perfect parent, but you will be who God created you to be to the very best of your ability, without the expectation of perfection. Accept where you are, accept your weaknesses, and trust God to be with you and provide for you all that you need and all your children need. We don't need a different situation or circumstance. We need to trust God.

In Isaiah 38:5 we read as Hezekiah is pleading with God. God has told him to prepare himself for death and to make arrangements for a successor to his throne. Hezekiah doesn't want this to be the situation, and he pleads with God. He begs for more time. He avoids the hard spot and the difficult situation. God gives Hezekiah fifteen more years to live, and in those years, Manasseh is born. Manasseh eventually is the ruler of Judah and is so evil and wicked that he provokes God and leads to Judah's eventual fall to the Babylonians. If Hezekiah had simply faced the difficult situation and lowered his head and gone through it instead of asking to avoid it, the history of an entire nation would read differently.

We need to accept our weaknesses and our situations and count on God's wisdom and strength. Additionally, we have to realize that at times, our struggles, our difficult times, and our tears are bringing glory to God in ways we will never know. All we can do is pray for endurance and the wisdom to go where God leads. We are often ones who can feel a lot like Job, wounded, destroyed in many ways, yet able to bring glory to God because we realize we did not lay the foundations of the universe. We realize we do not have all the answers, and we realize that as we struggle, God's strength shows. We will never know what that really looks like to our children. At our lowest times, if we watch carefully, we can count on God to give us a glimpse to carry us through.

One evening I was having a hard time. I was simply just too tired and overwhelmed by the demands on my time and energy. It was time to take my son to an athletic practice, and I was trying to finish laundry and clean up from dinner, slip in some exercise for myself, and pack up some supplies from work needing my attention during the practice because I had not had time during the workday to finish it. I was feeling totally beat by life. As we gathered things and headed for the car, my son noticed I was on the verge of tears. He asked what was wrong, and my only response was "I don't know, Son." It was far too much to dump on a teenage boy. He hugged me and then he told me about a discussion in his church small group. They each had been asked to tell the group about someone who inspires them. My son said that he told the group about me. He said he told them that he sees that sometimes I am so tired and there is so much to do, but no matter what, I just push on and get what must be done taken care of. He told me I inspire him! My fifteen-year-old son told me I inspire him! What a gift from God—and something I had no idea God was doing with my hard days when I had to grind through the piles of responsibilities and push on when I felt too weak. Truly my weakness and God's strength was accomplishing far more than I imagined.

Our great days and happy days will outnumber our days of struggle. That is the joy of the Lord! Our days of struggle and our weaknesses are where the power of God shines brightly and we glorify him in our willingness to simply grind on through the hard stuff. In the midst of our rebuilding of our city wall—the rebuilding of our lives—we need to keep our focus on the importance of the building of our children and the strength God offers us to accomplish this. We need to willingly accept that we have weaknesses and that we need the power of God to shine through those. We gain so much when we accept that our children need to learn forgiveness, humility, and reliance on God more than they need a perfect parent.

Our Children Are Going to Ask Questions

When he was twelve years old, they went up to the festival, according to the custom. After the festival was over, while his parents were returning home, the boy Jesus stayed behind in Jerusalem, but they were unaware of it. Thinking he was in their company, they traveled on for a day. Then they began looking for him among their relatives and friends. When they did not find him, they went back to Jerusalem to look for him. After three days they found him in the temple courts, sitting among the teachers, listening to them and asking them questions.

—Luke 2:42–46 (NIV)

We all can connect with the moments when our young child asks more questions than we can imagine answering, and all in one short run to the grocery store. We know that learning and asking questions are inseparable, so we delight in the questions of our little ones. As they grow older, the questions change or sometimes stop altogether. Either one of those scenarios can be challenging and difficult for us as parents. We should embrace the challenging and difficult questions, even the questions that leave us without an answer. We need to be purposeful to cultivate a relationship with our children that will prevent the questions from stopping.

The most important question we need to answer first is this: are you comfortable with knowing you will not always have the answers to all your child's questions? We need to recognize we are not perfect and that we will encounter questions from our children that leave us without an answer. We need to become comfortable with our limitations in order to keep the lines of communication open with our children. We want our children to come to us with all their questions, even those beyond our ability to answer. Through prayer, honesty, and sometimes research, we can allow our children to ask us all their questions and help them move into young adulthood with a confidence in themselves and their beliefs.

At some point your children will start to ask questions about their faith. I actually found this to be an exciting time because I knew my children wanted to own their faith for themselves. When they were small children, we attended church together, and I would take them to Sunday school. They simply believed what they heard. As they grew and began to ask questions, I knew they were starting to analyze and genuinely decide what they would take into their hearts and what they would not. The struggles when they chose to reject an ideal I held were real. In those struggles, my children came to own deep within their own hearts a set of faith ideals that generated the depth of faith I had prayed for them to gain.

When my children began asking questions, I intentionally tried to be open to conversation with them and allow ideas that seemed completely out of my faith perspective to be heard and discussed. I didn't want to establish an atmosphere that would cause my children to think they had to agree with me. I wanted to nurture an environment encouraging of conversation and questions without fear of judgment. Sometimes the conversations seemed to take some extremely interesting twists and turns. In the end, when conclusions were measured against scripture, we would all find that the questions and conversations refined our beliefs and stretched our understandings in ways that helped us each to grow. I genuinely found my faith growing as I watched my children explore and claim their beliefs for themselves.

I will admit, often they would ask questions I was not sure I could answer. If I had an answer, I honestly gave it. If we disagreed, I allowed them to discuss their thoughts and treated their ideas with respect and grace. If I did not have an answer, I was honest and told them I did not have an answer. Some faith questions don't have definitive answers. Faith is not something we gain from a simple answer. Faith believes there is an answer, even if we don't know it or get to know it.

In the book of Job, we find a man of faith who has encountered tragedy after tragedy in his life. He takes his questions directly to God. That act—taking one's questions to God—is an act of faith. Job recognizes that God is the source of knowledge and is the one place where the answers can or should be found. After Job asks God his questions, God answers with "Where were you when I laid the earth's foundation? Tell me, if you understand" (Job 38:4 NIV). Job asks questions and gets an answer that is not an answer at all. Job is told he is not God and he isn't going to understand. The answer Job gets is one we also get at times when we explore and strive to understand the mysteries of faith. There will be times when we need to tell our children the answers that they are seeking are in the same category—ones that will not generate a simple or humanly comprehensible answer. As we strive to gain depth and understanding for our faith, we will not always get an answer. As our children strive to gain depth and understanding for their faith, they will not always get an answer. Faith empowers us to believe without fully understanding because we were not there when God laid the foundations of the universe.

I find comfort in the book of Job for a few reasons. We learn through the questions Job takes to God that God is not bothered by our questions or the questions our children bring. I also gain comfort in knowing it is a normal part of our human condition to ask questions. Most important for my resolve as a parent, I see I should not have all the answers to all the questions my children will ask. Sometimes the answer is simply that God is God and we don't understand. I have found that as I accept I may not have the answers to all the questions my children ask, I can give them room to question and even express doubt more freely. Those questions and doubts represent struggle as children seek to own their faith. It isn't wrong to struggle. Struggle will produce deep, real faith. When we allow our children to ask probing questions, we will then know that they are striving to establish a depth of faith that will result in great joy as they grow older. Those probing questions will require thought from us as we respond. We can't lead our children to a deep faith by giving them platitudes and simple answers. On the contrary, we may have to jump into the struggle with them at times as we seek to find the answers for ourselves. All of this is healthy and generates a stronger faith that will stand up to the storms of life. Our children will possess a more mature faith that knows what it holds dear and is worth fighting for. They will also learn what is not significant and not worth fighting for.

The beauty of the questions is that they launch amazing conversations. In these conversations we learn who our children are on a faith level, and they learn who we are on a faith level as well. We can become the support system for our children as they strive to live out the faith issues they deem to be worth fighting for. We can become partners in assisting them to live out a faith they have sorted through and now hold in their hearts. We move from the author and enforcer of rules to the supporter of a living faith they have chosen for themselves. They begin to live out their faith in a life of holiness. Holiness is not reserved for the most pious. It is for those who have allowed growth as a disciple of Christ to change who they are and how they do their daily living. Holiness is a way of living and is the way we demonstrate our faith to those we encounter in our daily lives. This depth of faith permeates how we live daily and is what we want our children to cultivate through questions and discovery.

While we nurture an atmosphere that welcomes questions and empowers discussions about faith, we should hope that those faith questions will lead to life questions as well. Our children are saturated with images through media and social media that are unsettling and disturbing. They are exposed to far more than their developing emotional states can process. They will be confused, and they will need guidance and help to sort through the conflicting and disturbing images and circumstances they encounter every day. We need to make certain we have established an open dialogue that welcomes questions and discussions on absolutely every topic. We need to accept that avoiding a topic because it is uncomfortable to us, or because it is something we would not have discussed with our own parents, is not good parenting. We need to be able to have the conversations and allow our children to ask the questions that living in this social media–saturated culture generates. We do not want to shut down the difficult topics or give our children "discussion closed" responses to the confusion and struggles they encounter. If we are not the source of information and a safe place for discussion, they will take their questions to someone else. When that happens, you may not appreciate the information they gather or the opinions that shape their thinking.

This is hard, and I can't claim I always handled it well. I have heard my own children tell me I don't understand. I heard my own children say I did not listen and was too closed-minded. And I was honestly trying not to be closed-minded or opinionated. We all have opinions, and we all desire what we know is best for our children. The delicate balance between leading them to discover the "best for them" answer without seeming closed-minded and not being permissive and weak is not a balance I always managed. I don't know if any parent manages that balance well all of the time. What we can do is try. Again, be honest with your children when you fail.

One topic I struggle with most is drug use. When my children want to discuss and ask questions about drug use, I do not manage an open-minded, rational demeanor. I have seen in the lives of people I love the horrible effects of addiction, and I have an emotional response to drug use. I don't even come close to staying calm and presenting an open-minded conversation on the topic. I tell my children why. I speak honestly with them about my emotional response and share facts as best I can. When they observe my emotional responses, they know it is not because of their questions but because of my emotions. It has preserved the honest communication I have worked hard to build between me and my children.

If you establish an atmosphere of safe and honest communication, your children will ask you questions about absolutely everything because they are exposed to absolutely everything through social media. Gone are the days when your children could be sheltered and only see the PG versions of shows and life. There simply is not a way to manage all the images and input coming at our children. If you have done a good job of making it safe for them to ask questions and engage in discussions without feeling judged, you will field questions on topics you never imagined talking to your children about. Know this is a good thing. You want your children to come to you as the place to talk, ask, discuss, and learn. You want them to collect the answers about life and about living life consistently with their faith from you. I am always saddened when I hear a teen say, "I could never talk to my parents about that." This means the young person is getting answers from a variety of sources, most of which won't be supportive of a faith-based response.

When your children start asking questions, take a deep breath and really listen. Listen not just to the question itself but also to what is generating the question, if you can discern it. Is it fear your child is feeling, or lack of self-esteem? Perhaps your child wishes to fit in with certain students, or perhaps he is attempting to understand why he feels that he should not fit in with friends who have started to make choices he doesn't want to make. Behind the questions are feelings and reasons for asking. Listen for those reasons, and you will find your emotional response tempered. The last thing you want to do is make your children feel they can't bring you a question.

One key component to this is trust. If your children confide in you, be trustworthy. Don't discuss with other parents the topics of conversation you have with your children. You want your children to feel you are a safe place to come with questions, a person they can trust with their doubts. The only time you should ever violate the trust of your child is in the event of a topic that reveals your child is contemplating self-harm or harm to others. Other than that circumstance, the contents of your conversations with your children must remain confidential.

Another practice to help nurture an open conversational atmosphere is providing purposeful responses. It is natural to gasp at some of the things our children encounter. We want to simply say, "Things should not be that way, and you are forbidden to do that." When our children are grown enough to bring topics to us that make us gasp, they are too grown for us to simply force our solution. We need to internalize the gasp, pause, pray, and listen more than we talk. We also need to avoid the standard responses that cause our children to cringe. You know what responses I am talking about. Don't let yourself say, "Well, when I was a kid, that just didn't happen" or "Good kids just don't do those things." Your children don't need to be told how it has to be; they need you to be open and honest with them. Discuss the pitfalls and dangers by asking them to identify the dangers. Share with them the emotional impact of actions. Tell your son that when he holds a girl's hand, he is also holding that girl's heart. Tell your daughters that physical attention from a boy is not emotional connection. Give them the real facts. Discuss the physical impact of not taking care of their bodies through chemical abuse. Learn about the dopamine effect and how addiction stems from this so you can share and discuss facts with your children. Use questions such as, "Do you see the dangers in that?" "Do you know what that would do to that person?" "Do you realize the results of getting caught up in that?" and "Do you know what you have to lose?" Use real-life examples to show them the answers to those questions. Don't just resort to quick judgments, but rather lead your children through discussion and questions, helping them find the answers that make for sound and healthy judgments they can own for themselves. These will become convictions they will choose to live by. Open discussion allows them to generate convictions that are true to who they understand themselves to be, reflecting the faith they have established. Through questions and discussions of faith, they will have a solid faith shaping the convictions they establish as they confront the cultural and social questions that seem overwhelming to us.

> He will sit as a refiner and purifier of silver; he will
> purify the Levites and refine them like gold and silver.
> Then the Lord will have men who will bring offerings
> in righteousness. (Malachi 3:3 NIV)

I had a wonderful conversation with a close friend about this verse. I learned that while silver is in the furnace for refining, it must be watched carefully. If the amount of time required to refine silver is exceeded by the smallest fraction, the silver is damaged. The silversmith knows the refining is completed when he can see his own image in the silver. Then he knows the process is complete. In this conversation she was reflecting on the amazing power of God to refine each of us. I realized later this refining is a lot like the questions our children will ask. It is our job to guide them through refining their faith and understanding their place in this world as disciples by teaching them to test their beliefs in the purifying fires and look for a reflection that looks like a disciple of Christ. Sometimes we fear the heat of the refining fires, but we should recognize it as a part of the process necessary for the metal to shine and the reflection of a disciple to emerge.

God knows we are in the fire, and he is watching over the refining process. We can be confident that he sits and keeps watch, waiting until his reflection is visible in our lives. We need to embrace the questions of our children and the opportunities to guide them as they refine their faith and learn to live their faith daily.

There is one other benefit to creating a relationship with our children that empowers them to ask questions and have important discussions. We teach them to ask questions and communicate so that as they mature, they can take this skill into adult life and adult relationships. It is important to help them transfer the communication skills they learn in conversations with us to conversations with authority figures in their lives. As we teach them to ask questions and have respectful conversations, we are preparing them with a valuable skill.

In our conversations with our children, we need to teach them how to ask questions. We need to instill in our children an attitude of gratitude and respect toward those who teach them, coach them, and lead them. A vital part of that is to teach them to respectfully ask questions and raise concerns with these people when they need to. This can be challenging for our children. I know for my children, growing up without a dad led both of them to struggle with questioning or communicating with men. I needed to actively guide them through some of these conversations when they were young so they would gain confidence in their ability to ask questions when needed. Simple awareness of the potential struggle made it possible for me to help them overcome this struggle. We need to recognize that our children are not naturally going to communicate well. We do need to guide them and teach them how to communicate in a healthy and productive manner. This learning process can begin by establishing a healthy atmosphere for questions and discussions with us. It may be hard to believe, but a healthy atmosphere for questions starts with the flood of questions from your young child on the way to the grocery store.

GOD'S GOT THIS

But blessed is the one who trusts in the lord, whose confidence is in him. They will be like a tree planted by the water that sends out its roots by the stream. It does not fear when heat comes; its leaves are always green. It has no worries in a year of drought and never fails to bear fruit.

—Jeremiah 17:7–8 (NIV)

We are never prepared for the struggles that come. We know there will be struggles, but we don't know exactly what they will look like. As life moves along, we can catch glimpses of what those struggles might look like, but until we are living them, we aren't really clear what they will be like. Sometimes our fear of the struggle coming is greater than the struggle itself. Other times, we are hit with a struggle we didn't see coming at all. Regardless, there is really no way to be completely prepared. The one thing that is a constant is that we can turn to God to guide us, provide what we need, and comfort us in the hardest times.

We do not have to generate our own solutions and solve our own problems. We may want to spring into action and get on track quickly to fix all that seems to present a challenge or a struggle. At times, though, that is the easy way out. We need to be honest with ourselves and admit that when we do spring into action to fix things our way, the result is usually a bit of a mess. When we place our hope in God and wait for direction and guidance from God, the solutions are better than what we would have created for ourselves. It is honestly easier to spring into action and do something, anything, to fix things. Action is easier than being still and waiting for God to lead us to the very best solution.

When the struggles come, we have a chance to show our children a way to live through those struggles by teaching them through our own action how to respond in faith. Faith responses are a key component to raising children with God as the head of the household. We want our children to live a faith-driven life, so we must model faith responses as we raise them. We must train ourselves to respond to all circumstances through faith. We also must be purposeful to share our prayers about and our thoughts on these responses with our children so they can learn to do the same when they encounter struggles.

In Luke chapter 8, we read of a set of faith responses that I think model our task as parents very well. The focus of my point is found beginning in verse 40 and continuing through verse 50. Jesus is moving through a crowd when Jairus, the synagogue leader, comes to Jesus because his daughter is sick and dying. He is requesting that Jesus heal her. Right here we have a huge act of prideless faith! Jairus is the synagogue leader! He is going out into public to ask for a miracle from Jesus, who has not been accepted as the Messiah by the synagogue leadership. Jairus, not concerned with his own status, or appearance to others—and there were a lot of others; a huge crowd had formed around Jesus—goes forward in an act of faith for his daughter's sake. Now while Jairus is making a public statement of faith for his daughter's sake, a woman who should not be in the crowd at all is trying to gain healing for herself from an affliction that has kept her isolated and apart from society for years. Believing she will be healed leads her to an equally huge act of faith. She is going against all societal rules to be there in that crowd. She believes Jesus can heal her, so she pushes through the crowd simply to touch his robe. She believes by faith in Jesus this is her chance to be healed. She is healed, and Jesus's words to her are "Daughter your faith has healed you. Go in peace" (Luke 8:48 NIV). As Jesus then continues on, a message comes to the crowd that Jairus's daughter has died. This is when Jesus speaks the words to Jairus that are for us to engrave on our hearts. He says, "Don't be afraid; just believe, and she will be healed" (Luke 8:50 NIV).

Please don't think I am indicating that all our children's illnesses can be healed by faith alone. I am not addressing medical issues. I am looking at our parental responses to the constant litany of challenges that face our homes and families. In each one we should hear Jesus saying to us,

"Don't be afraid; just believe." We must believe God wants the very best for his children, including the ones we are in charge of raising in our homes. God wants to provide for them the best way to use their talents; the best relationships for them to love, be loved, and share their faith; and a way for them to experience the best life situations. This does not always mean we will like the circumstances or lessons they must endure to arrive at God's very best. There will be times when God's very best takes longer to arrive than we want, seems harder to attain than we wish it would be, or involves hardships we don't want our children to have to endure. At each of those turns, we must continue to respond with no fear; we must live our faith and step forward in faith like Jairus and the woman in Luke! These powerful words direct our responses to all of the challenges we face, big and small: *Do not be afraid; just believe!*

In those times when we feel fear creeping in, we need to look to scripture with the perspective offered by Henry Blackaby: "When God speaks about His plans, He does so with everything already in place to fulfill His word."[2]

Do we believe this deep in our hearts? We should, and reflecting on scripture with this perspective will add depth to our belief. As we look at the life of Joseph (found in the book of Genesis), we see so many times when fear and disappointment would be natural. However, God led Joseph to the place where he was to be to fulfill God's plan. As the Hebrew people survived slavery and Moses fled to Midian, fear and loss of hope would be natural. God had plans for a nation promised to Abraham, and all of these events in the lives of Joseph and Abraham were a part of the plan. When Mary was visited by an angel, the impossible was foretold, but again scripture shows us hundreds of years of history passing between the time of the prophecy and the visit by an angel. This examination of scripture shows us how God put so much in place to lead to the birth of the Messiah. All Mary had to do when she experienced the visit from an angel was believe.

When our children are born, an immense love fills our hearts and becomes nearly overwhelming. We see the talents God places in our

---

[2] H. Blackaby and R. Blackaby, *Experiencing God Day by Day* (Nashville: B&H Books, 2006), 375.

children and watch their personalities emerge and then mature. We can't help ourselves; we want what they want. We want to see the goals and dreams God plants in their hearts realized. We want to help. In some cases we want to help, support, cheer, and do everything to make things happen for our children. In the midst of that, we can inadvertently move from loving, guiding, and supporting them to a place that is overbearing—"helicopter-parent-like," faithless parenting. I have watched parents completely lose track of their children in the pursuit of the dreams they believe their children hold in their hearts. As they pursue all the best avenues and opportunities for their children, they become a demonstration of self-driven pursuits, instead of leading their children to be faith-driven disciples who seek to do all they can to become who God created them to be. We seem to forget our children are God's children and that God has everything in place. God has it all worked out already.

My son went through a three-year stretch of injuries and struggles with a sport he was extremely passionate about. In the earlier chapter on humility, I shared this, but it is worth repeating. As he went through physical therapy and struggled to regain his ability to play, he was blessed by a young coach who taught him to pray daily a simple prayer: "Thank you, God, for what you have done in my life and what you will do!" My son had significant disappointments and injuries during those three years. He had many reasons to lose hope and let go of the faith telling him God was at work in his life. As we prayed this prayer every night, we both gained conviction in our faith response. Every time we would pray together, we would affirm our hope and faith that God was at work and that God had everything in place. We would thank God for the good in our lives and make our requests, and my son would end with that simple prayer. When the injuries had healed and the growing pains stopped, we were able to look back over those years and see what God was doing. My son now has a strong body, great skill and determination, and a Christ-centered, faith-based coach who believes in what he can do now and sees what God can do with him in the future. That is what God was doing. God had everything in place for the near future, and I know God has everything in place for the distant future for my children as well. Faith in God's plan, reinforced by daily prayer, was the constant through that struggle.

> And we know that in all things God works for the good
> of those who love him, who have been called according
> to his purpose. (Romans 8:28 NIV)

My experiences are not rare or unique. God is at work for the good of all his children. I have a dear friend who is married to an air force officer. Life in our military means a lot of moves from one base to another. While her family was stationed in Abilene, Texas, her youngest son enjoyed playing football in his first years of high school. Then they were moved to another state where he was not able to play football. The young man made the most of his time in this area and cross-trained and worked on his strength and conditioning. Living only by faith in the matter of his athletics, he pressed forward, working out and gaining strength. I am certain his mom, my dear friend, hurt for her son as she watched him hurt over not having a chance to play football. Then, her husband was deployed and the family moved back to Abilene for the boy's senior year in high school. No one could have known he would be able to play football his senior year among friends and be stronger and more fit than he expected to be. God had worked out such an amazing experience for his faith-filled young disciple. Not only did this young man play with friends who were also faith-filled young men, but also they went all the way to the Texas State Championship game, and he played in the Dallas Cowboys home stadium for that game. While my friend was hurting for her child, she could never have imagined God was working out this kind of experience for her son.

I have watched parents work diligently to access opportunities for their children only to have all the plans they struggled to put in place crumble. I have also watched parents strive to help their children live by faith and diligently work to better their skills and abilities, and then end up watching them access opportunities they could not have imagined would be offered their children.

When my son began high school, I was feeling overwhelmed with the calendar he was filling up fast. As the freshman-year football season started, I worried, looked at the calendar as it filled, organized, planned, and did all I could to figure it all out. He had the opportunity to train with varsity, which was a fantastic opportunity, but also there were soccer tournaments, and it looked like a real struggle was looming. God had it all in place. He has all our children's futures established if we will trust him, follow him, and walk in faith. If we do this, then God will take care of the rest better than we can! Because of some issues I knew nothing about, all of the potential conflicts simply disappeared. All my worry was wasted energy. God had it all worked out. This is what we need to know deep in our hearts. God has got this—even if we can't see a solution or generate a plan. God's plan is not just for our children—he has our futures in place too! Walk in faith. Follow him, and he will show you how it is all established for our very best. God will do what is best for your children and for you if you allow his leading and accept his time line. The most unexpected and even unwanted things turn out to be huge blessings from God.

A key aspect of this is obedience. I am not referring to your children's obedience to you. I am referring to your obedience to God. God knows the long-range plan and the vision for the future. God gives directives to us, and it is our task to obey. This is uncomfortable language for most of us. The honest truth is that we are servants, and Christ is not only our Savior but also our Lord. We are to his seek direction and obey him. When our children watch this process in our lives, they are more likely to follow the directive of God in faith as well. When you honestly and wholeheartedly ask God what he wants of you, he will answer you so you will know. He will make it known to you either through a prompting of the Holy Spirit, through a burning bush experience, through a still small voice, or through an event that generates understanding. God wants you to know, and more, God wants you to obey.

Obeying is tricky. It's not that we don't know what God wants of us; it's that we often don't want to do it. We will be convinced by our culture and the worldly approach that obeying God will be too costly. The world will tell us there is a simple fast track and that we don't have to obey God and do what he is directing us to do. Our culture will tell us that we can't have joy in obedience to God. But the reality is, without obeying God, abundant joy is not possible. When we make faith responses our standard, we have hope and hold real joy—not circumstantial joy, but real genuine joy! We have the promise of our God's presence and guidance and can respond to the daily struggles of life with hope and confidence in our God.

Walking obediently in faith helps us recognize there are several roads that go to the same place. Often we hear the discussions and counsel of those who "know" how to help our children get to whatever goals they have in their hearts. Don't allow conventional wisdom to cause you to move your child off the path God is guiding them to travel on. The road for your child may not be what is viewed by others as the best route. Keep your children on the route that is best for them and the route designed by God. When I was in high school, the standard process to get into college was to plan ahead, apply early, have and strong grades and a strong extracurricular activity resume. I had the extracurricular activities and somewhat strong grades but no planning ahead. As fall approached, I was starting to wonder what God was doing with me. I had applied to a few schools I hoped to attend and had not been accepted. When I was thinking there was no hope, God taught me he doesn't show up late. In two days I went from having no plan to packing my things and heading to the best college for my talents and God's plan for my future.

I am not saying we can just relax and do nothing and God will take care of everything. We still need to teach our children to be good stewards of their talents, establish a strong work ethic, and be diligent in discerning God's direction and will for their lives. We do not have to think that there is only one way to accomplish the goals our children have set.

Google Maps takes you the fastest route and gives you a couple of options. After driving a tremendous number of miles one summer, I often found these "fastest route" roads are congested, slow, and frustrating. No matter how hard you try, you can't make Google Maps choose the scenic route. There are multiple ways to get into a town, and sometimes the scenic route is the best one to take. For your child, there are multiple roads to travel to higher education, musical and artistic accomplishments, athletic accomplishments, and all other life achievements they are drawn toward. Trust that God has it all worked out. God has placed talents and abilities within your child for a higher purpose than you can imagine. God wants your child to shine and be a strong witness for the goodness of God. If you find God has placed your child on a "scenic route," teach your child to look around, take in the beauty, and learn from the experiences found on that route. The road less traveled is often the road that makes all the difference. ("Two roads diverged in a wood and I—I took the one less traveled by, and that has made all the difference." —Robert Frost)

Our task as parents is a hard one. Parental pride can blind us to what God is doing to give our children his very best. We need to hold strong to our faith, make our spiritual growth a priority, and make our children's spiritual growth a priority. We need to intentionally reject the cultural expectations and bragging of other parents. We need to keep our eyes focused on who God has created our children to be, not how many trophies, ribbons, or awards they amass. If we are counting awards and listening to the applause of the crowd, we will lose the ability to hear the voice of God as he guides our parenting and guides the steps of our children. We need to learn to keep our eyes on Christ and stay focused on him. It is easy and tempting to allow the standards and draw of this world's sparkle, shine, and prestige to affect what we deem important. Nothing is as valuable as our ability to hear God's leading voice—to be able to follow God so we can make the wise choices for our children (and for ourselves).

If we place what God values at the top of our priority list, we are going to begin making choices and decisions that are in contrast to what the world applauds. This is where the practice of obedience becomes an important part of what our children witness. Not only will they see us acting in faith, but also they will witness that they can trust God for the outcome as well. Each time we trust and walk by faith, and each time God provides and leads us to a better outcome than we could have generated, our children learn God is able to provide our every need. We need to be conscious to articulate to our children that there is a difference between what we need and what we want. As we seek to live in obedience to Christ's leading, what we want soon becomes more like what God is providing anyway. When we maintain our obedience to Christ and our thankfulness for what is provided, our children will experience and know they can trust God to provide every need. They will see through us that the greatest things to value are those that God is providing. As they grow to value what God values, they are rooted in a heart-deep understanding that God does indeed have this!

So often we are in the place Moses found himself when God spoke to him. Moses was busy—he was at work trying to track down a wayward sheep. Doesn't this sound all too familiar to a parent? In the midst of his search for the wayward sheep, Moses encountered the burning bush. Moses thought he was simply doing his job but discovered he was on holy ground. We must realize we are also on holy ground. Parenting with God as the coparent of our children is nothing less than standing on holy ground every day. Granted, when you are changing diapers, picking up many brightly colored plastic toys at night, tutoring homework and study time, or listening to the complaints of a moody teenager, it doesn't exactly feel holy. I assure you, this phase of our lives is very holy ground. We are in partnership with God, guiding the children he has blessed us with into not just adulthood but also the adult life God had in mind when he created them. It is hard to imagine what their adult lives will look like. One thing I do know for sure is this: God has got this! We are in partnership with the One who laid the foundation of the universe. He can certainly guide me to handle my strong-willed children.

When Moses found himself on holy ground, God spoke a message unique to him. The first thing Moses heard was his own name. I often wonder if Moses had not been alone on the mountain, would the other shepherds working in the area have noticed the burning bush? Would they have heard God's voice? The message that day was uniquely for Moses. Would someone else have heard and understood? I don't think so. I think any possible spectators would not have understood the backwards path Moses was led to take. I think they would have looked at the unconventional plan to abandon the family business and return to a country where he was considered a criminal as nothing short of insanity. Most likely, not only would they have not understood, but also they would have tried to talk Moses out of believing he saw the burning bush or heard God's directive at all. When God speaks to us, it is unique for just us individually. Others around us may not hear. It is to call and guide us individually.

How often do we let the standards of our culture and the voices all around us convince us we are nothing short of insane and persuade us that we should dismiss the callings or leadings we think we hear? We absolutely are living on holy ground, and the leadings are as important for our children as they were for the Israelites when Moses was talking to a burning bush. We need to listen and know where God sends us. God will also provide for us what is needed. As stated earlier, God has the future details worked out as clearly as our memory of the past. God has got this, our children's past, present, and future—and ours too.

I also wonder if Moses had passed by burning bushes before this one and perhaps didn't notice them. I think it is entirely possible we miss burning bushes all the time. I am fairly certain that far too often I get caught up in my list of to-do items and miss the burning bush messages because they don't make the "urgent and important" list I am keeping. I don't take time to look away from all the tasks I expend energy on to notice a burning bush opportunity.

If we keep the knowledge in mind that God has got things worked out ahead of us, and if we know that our most important task is to listen to God and follow where he leads us, we won't miss the miraculous moments God has set in place for us. We need to seek God's direction and advice constantly so his leading is the primary source for the decisions we make for our children and for ourselves. Knowing that God wants to speak to us, we should move through our days anticipating an encounter with a burning bush. We should watch for moments when God will speak and provide direction. Additionally, we need to be prepared to stop—get off our predetermined path—and listen. When Moses saw the burning bush, he paused. He stopped what he was doing—he quit searching for the lost sheep. When we think we are in the presence of a burning bush, we need to stop as well. We need to stop searching for, or trying to generate, our own solution. We need to stop looking for the lost sheep we think is missing in our lives. We need to stop looking at our list of what needs to be done and, instead, look to God. We need to stop and step toward the burning bush—and listen.

Look at what God is doing. Hear what God is saying. Allow God to be the lead parent and authority in the decisions you are making for yourself and for your children. This will ensure your children have the best possible parent! Stop, listen, and follow God to establish him as the head of the household in your home, which will make it easier to help your children understand God is the provider. It is easy in today's culture for our children to think of themselves as the source of their own talents, gifts, and accomplishments. There is nothing further from truth. The truth is, God is the source of all the talents, gifts, and graces your children enjoy.

As often as your children enjoy accolades or accomplishments, remind them that the source of the talent at the foundation of that accomplishment is God. Focus their attention on the abundant joy they feel when they are enjoying that talent. Tell them how you have seen them glorify God with the talent they have used. Remind them that how they use the talent is as important as what they accomplish with the talent.

It is easy to get on the quickest route to the goal, but we must remember the burning bush was not on the fastest route. The burning bush was along the scenic route during a detour in Moses's day. As we move along through our daily living, we need to remind ourselves and our children that the fastest route could cause us to miss the burning bush moments that clarify our tasks and purpose as well as the goal God is setting before us. It is a challenge to discern God's purpose for our lives, and it is certainly a weighty challenge to guide our children to discern God's purpose in their lives. This is the primary task we must strive to accomplish. We must be willing to discuss with our children God's purpose for the talents and gifts they possess. It is humbling and overwhelming when I talk with my children about the wonderful gifts God has blessed them with, framing the discussion in the context of what God created them to do for the kingdom. It is amazing to realize the precious children I am raising are created by a loving God who has something specific in mind for them. When we define successful parenting not by the number of awards our children win but rather by how well they see themselves as children of God with a unique set of gifts and talents combining to accomplish a God-given purpose, we are living on holy ground.

"Our Father who art in heaven, hallowed be thy name" translated means "God in heaven, your name should be glorified." Everyone, whether faith driven or not, seems to seek for purpose in life. We all want purpose in our lives. As faith-driven people, we strive to know what God wants of us and for us. The answer is as clear as the first line of the prayer Jesus taught his disciples. As individual Christians we are to bring glory to God. Our calling as parents is to bring glory to God so we enable our children to see the goodness of God. Further, we want to empower our children to know God as their loving heavenly Father so they will seek to glorify him as well. This is the purpose of a disciple. God does not just leave us to our own devices to glorify him. Rather, God blesses us with talents to guide us to find the ways in which we can fulfill our purpose.

It is important we have direct and purposeful conversations with our children about the gifts and talents they are blessed with and God's purpose for those gifts. One effective means to address this topic with children is the parable of the talents found in the Gospel of Matthew, chapter 25, verses 14–30. This parable can clearly teach that when God blesses us with ability or talent, we are to make use of it to glorify God. As my children have grown, the discussions of this parable have become more in depth. I may not always have the right words during these discussions, but I know I have my children realizing and thinking about the talents they are blessed with and the responsibilities those talents bring. Anytime we parents can use scripture to support the lessons we hope to teach our children, we should lead them to it and study it with them.

When I am seeking to fill my children's hearts with courage and confidence, I like to share stories from the book of Joshua. Caleb is a resource for any faith-driven person who is seeking an example of living the call of God in the face of challenges. Caleb knew what God expected of him. Caleb also knew God had been with him through so many challenges, and God was his source of strength. He trusted God as his strength and was willing to go into whatever battle or situation God led him to. If I can plant the faith shown by Caleb deep in my children's hearts, perhaps they will also be courageous and willing to face the challenges in front of them to follow where God leads.

We need to boldly teach our children that if they are to glorify God, they will need to be willing to go where God calls them and rely on divine strength, not the human strength and direction chosen by the people who seek applause, awards, and accolades. Teaching children to follow God into the challenges ahead depends on teaching them to understand God has the plan, the details, and the strength. God has got this. They need to trust and move forward. As we teach them God has got this, they come to know that when God gives them an assignment or a calling, they shouldn't waste time arguing with God over it or discussing why they think they can't accomplish it. We must make certain they know God doesn't place in front of them tasks they can accomplish on their own strength that would glorify them. Instead, God sets them on the path to accomplish that which could only be accomplished by the power of God. God wants to accomplish the impossible through them and through your life as their parent so that those who are witnessing are certain God deserves the glory.

When our children watch us face challenges with prayer and the faith of knowing God has got the outcome, they learn to rely on God's strength and resources instead of their own to overcome the challenges they face. We need to remind ourselves we are not alone and God is with us. The obstacle in front of you may seem insurmountable, but God is with you, and you are not handling it alone. We need to demonstrate this to our children as we face the inevitable challenges and obstacles ahead.

Significant to this process is trusting God for the outcome. We want our children to achieve, and we want to be able to give them all the resources and opportunities to do so. Sometimes that is not what is best for our children. God knows this. God has what is best for us and what is best for our children ahead as long as we strive to follow his leading and expressed will. A huge part of faith is following the will of God and trusting him for the outcome. If you look back on the path of your life, you will see places that seemed like obstacles or closed doors then but that now are clearly bridges and pathways to blessings. I know this is true for me and for my children. Trusting that God had the outcome has allowed obstacles and challenges to become blessings. Often when we parents feel we have failed to provide a resource or opportunity for our children, God will use the circumstance to generate a greater outcome than what we were trying to help them achieve. We need to trust God has got the outcome.

Our children gain strength in hard work and character through struggles. We don't help them by trying to fix every disappointment and by leading them to avoid obstacles. We do the best thing for our children when we lead them to put their hope in God, to trust God, and to seek his help. God will give them the tools—strength, perseverance, hope, wisdom, and resources—to handle those seemingly impossible

JULIE ANN ALLEN

situations. Our children will experience the same thing we have as we walked in faith through challenges. This is where God is glorified, where he can display to an unbelieving world that in our weakness, he is strong!

This may mean seeing our children feel disappointed at times. This may mean watching them not win a cross-country race or watching them lose a soccer game. This may mean they don't graduate in the top few in their high school class. This may mean having to tell them as a parent that you don't have the resources to access every advantage and opportunity they see other kids their age enjoying. God has got the outcome. So many of the closed doors I have experienced have been incredible blessings. So many of the disappointments and struggles I have comforted my children through have also turned out to be incredible blessings for them. I have learned the dark road can only be walked by faith and is the most blessed road to be traveling. Walking by faith can seem scary. Faith is a scary word! It takes courage to wait in faith. Moreover, acting in faith can lead us to places we never planned to go. Acting in faith can upset the apple cart of our lives.

> And without faith it is impossible to please God, because anyone who comes to him must believe that he exists and that he rewards those who earnestly seek him. (Hebrews 11:6–7 NIV)

As Hebrews addresses faith, there is a reference to Noah and the faith he demonstrated as he built the ark. I realize I have referenced Noah several times. There is a good reason. Here was a man called by God to build an enormous boat in an arid place. We can gain so much from studying Noah's story. When God instructed Noah to build a huge boat, Noah set out building right away. If Noah had waited for the rain to start before building, it would have been too late. I have no doubt that the need for a huge boat in a desert was not something his neighbors understood. When God places a call to action in our hearts, we need to act and not wait. As scary as it can be, we need to truly live our convictions. We must be ready to take risks, and we must have a mature faith that can endure God's "no" answers and redirections in our lives. We need to know we can trust God with the outcome. We can focus on the task God has set in front of us best when we accept that the final outcome is in God's hands—and that God has got this!

Walking in faith is scary, and trusting the outcome to God is difficult. Regardless, for the best outcome for our children and for ourselves, we need to do just that. We need to trust the seasons, timing, and outcome to God. Too often we try to force our time line or our solution instead of enjoying the season and the task God is calling us to accomplish. God has given you this task and this time in your life, so trust God to deal with the seasons, the timing, and the outcome. Live by faith today. Savor the moments, the people, the relationships, and the task you have today! It won't be long before this task will be a treasured memory. For this time while your children are in your home, you are the one God will use to show them faith is doing what you know to be the will of God and then trusting God for the outcome. Often doing what is best for our kids is counter to what the world says to do. When we know it is God's will to make certain decisions, we need to live those decisions for the sake of our children regardless of the appearance.

I can imagine that Noah had questions during the long task of building while he endured mocking from his community. I also imagine there were some questions during the long time spent floating in the storm. We are not that different from Noah in this. When we step out in faith, we have questions in our hearts. When those questions involve our children, they seem to dominate our thoughts. If we continue to practice our faith walk, and study and focus on the faithful acts of those we read about in scripture, we will have confidence and hope greater than the questions. Faith tells us God did not put us here to play it safe and to do the sure thing. He calls us to build a giant boat in the desert. Isn't that what parenting is? We step out in faith and go against what the common conventions say is the way to get ahead. We teach our children to strive for a stronger discipleship instead of working for applause. We try to lead them to find their identity in the title "child of God" instead of in the acclaim of our culture. When our questions push in, we gain strength from reading again the story of a mom who put her baby in a basket and set it afloat on the Nile. We can study the life of Abraham, who waited for a child and then walked him up a mountain, knowing God would deliver. We can reflect on the story of a Roman soldier who goes into a crowd to ask for healing for his daughter. Parenting is a daily act of faith—so we must seek God first and then parent our children.

Parenting can lead us to acts of faith that seem beyond our strength and into situations that seem beyond our resources. If we rely on only our own resources and strength, we don't learn to trust God. There is purpose in "give us this day our daily bread." Just as there was no way to stockpile manna in the desert, there is no way to stockpile security and certainty. We need to depend on God, not our stockpiles. God is aware of what tomorrow will bring and how we should prepare for it. God knows the problems we will face, and he has already put the provisions in place to help us overcome. We need faith in God today, and we also need to trust that he has our tomorrow in his hands. In the same vein, he has our children's futures in his hands, and we can trust Him for their futures—knowing even the struggles they are having today can be used for good by God.

But after I have risen, I will go ahead of you into Galilee.
(Mark 14:28 NIV)

Jesus tells his disciples even after he has been crucified and then resurrected that he will go ahead of them to Galilee. You can know God goes ahead of you in life. God is not going to send you somewhere he is not already going ahead of you. God is ahead of you in any situation you are in, and he is never surprised by what you are experiencing. God can meet your every need because he has gone before you and has already seen what is ahead of you. God waits, completely prepared to meet your needs only as God can do. Moreover, he is also beside you and with you providing comfort and protection as you move toward the places he is sending you. There is nowhere you can go where you will not find God is ahead of you and beside you as you go.

While parenting can seem overwhelming, God does not give us overwhelming circumstances. God gives us the strength so we can overcome those circumstances. As we look back on the adventure of parenting, we will see many situations are clearly the work of the hand of God. Modern miracles are visible when we look at the overwhelming situations that seemed to be resolved or conquered without our strength or control of them. These are the modern miracles that are a part of parenting when we allow God to be our children's parent. When Jesus performed many of his miracles, an action was required from the one healed. Jesus told people to go wash or pick up their bed or do some other action, and then overcoming of the overwhelming occurred. This is the same for us. When the call seems too daunting or too overwhelming, step forth in faith, and the miraculous overcoming will begin!

We need to know deep in our hearts that God has got all that overwhelms us and is prepared to lead us through the overcoming of all of it. More importantly, we need to know deep in our hearts that God has got all our children are facing and has a wonderful plan for their lives. We need to affirm to them that God has created them with unique talents and abilities to make an impact on the kingdom. Most importantly, we need to remind ourselves and our children that God has already gone ahead of us and has established provisions for all we will face as we move with God in faith.

We want to be the best parents ever! We all genuinely do. The fact is, we are human. In my classroom I have a part of a quote from Aristotle: "You are the sum of the choices you make." This is true about our parenting as well. We want to do the best we can, so we need to follow God's lead. We need to choose to do what God leads us to do and be the parents God guides us to be. We need to be who God calls us to be, and we need to go where, and do what, God leads us to on his command and at his time, not ours. This means acting in faith and not concerning ourselves with the appearances, social media bragging rights, or accepted practices of those around us. When we make the choice to let God be the guide for all our choices with our children, we will become the best parents for our children that God can provide.

THE CLIMB OUT ON THE WATER

"Come," he said. Then Peter got down out of the boat, walked on the water and came toward Jesus. But when he saw the wind, he was afraid and, beginning to sink, cried out, "Lord, save me!" Immediately Jesus reached out his hand and caught him. "You of little faith," he said, "why did you doubt?"

—Matthew 14:29–31 (NIV)

We can't see wind. What was Peter looking at when he saw the wind? Logic tells us he could see waves and other evidence of wind. I am certain there are scholarly discussions of this topic. In my experience, when I see evidence of wind, I become fearful. This is human nature. If the television station warns of possible ice and snow in Texas, there is frantic activity at the grocery store as people rush out to buy all they might need in the event of a storm. They are afraid they will have a need they won't be able to fulfill if ice covers the roads and makes them impassable. Often the expense of all those supplies is unnecessary as the storm is rarely as severe as our fears. I think a lot of the mistakes I have made as a parent were fueled by fears I generated by looking at the evidence of wind. This Matthew passage shows us that as long as we keep our eyes fixed on Jesus, we will do miraculous things. If we start looking at the signs of wind and storms and begin to sink, we only have to cry out to God, and he will reach out his hand and save us. There is a comforting message from this scripture as well. Peter is called "one with little faith." God used Peter in the early years of the church mightily. If Peter can demonstrate a lack of faith and still be a major part of the establishment of Christianity, then my lack of faith responses are not reasons for me to have a sense of failure.

So many aspects of single parenting feel like walking on water, with evidence of gale-force winds all around us. In my years as a single parent, I have seen so much evidence of wind, and I have also seen God lead me across some pretty stormy waters. I was having lunch with a very close friend who has known me for more than twenty-five years. She and I always talk authentically. During this lunch we did no different. She remarked on how amazed she was at my focus on God and dependence on him. She was praising my willingness to submit to his will in my life. I had to make a confession to her. When I am submitted to God's will, it is not because I am a paragon of discipleship—it's because I am scared and because I feel like I am out of the boat and don't want to sink.

As a teacher, I have seen so many examples of the incredible importance of parents in children's lives. I wish I could tell you there have been countless examples of wonderfully emotionally healthy children. Unfortunately, what I must tell you scares me so much as a parent, and especially as a single parent. There are not countless examples of emotionally healthy children. I am scared because I have seen classrooms full of broken children, students damaged by the selfish and mindless actions of parents who are seeking to take care of themselves first. The truth is that too few parents realize that if they mess up as a parent, they negatively impact the lives of their children and damage them. I am not talking about the small incidents like when you forget to send lunch money to school. I am talking about the consistent practice of putting your wants and even your needs ahead of the good of your children. When I hear a parent say, "Oh, kids are resilient," I think that most likely they are trying to justify allowing a damaging situation into the lives of their children. Those times when you do what is convenient or comfortable for you instead of doing what you know is best for your children are times that genuinely do damage to your children. I see classrooms where the majority of the students are emotionally destitute and the emotionally healthy children are the exception, not the rule. This is not only children of single parents or children of blended family settings. This is something that has no set family construct. As single parents, we must be vigilant to guard against this approach to parenting.

It would seem the one common trait shared by the children who are emotionally destitute is parenting based in self. Further, the one trait the emotionally healthy children seem to share is parenting genuinely based in seeking God as the head of the household, with the parent(s) genuinely seeking God to lead. It is a household pure in spirit, motivated by wanting to please God first.

Seeing this in my classrooms scared me. When I realized I was facing parenting two children alone, the fear changed the way I approached parenting. There simply was not room for self-serving actions or self-directed approaches. The weight of my children's futures completely anchored me to their heavenly Father. The honest truth is that I am not incredibly obedient to God; I am incredibly scared I am going to fail my children miserably and add more hurt and pain to their already hurt-filled lives.

Understand this very important thought: you are making disciples so they can then go out and make more disciples. God has created your children with unique gifts and talents to allow them to have an impact for the kingdom. Parenting your children is about helping them become who God created them to be and helping them find the abundant joy that comes from embracing their title of "child of God." Too often we think of situations in respect to ourselves. We are influenced by our needs, our loneliness, our hurts, or our desires for affirmation. For this time, this season, it is about your child or children. This season of life is going to pass so quickly. I have been raising my children as a widowed single mom for sixteen years so far. When I held my infant son and looked at my seven-year-old daughter after their father had died, I honestly thought there was no way I could run this race God had set in front of me. It was too long, and I knew I could not do it. Now that seven-year-old daughter is grown and establishing her own home, and that infant son is nearly through high school. And oh what I would give to have one more read through *Guess How Much I Love You* on the couch with the two of them beside me. I still have a couple of years with my son in high school, but I am already missing the days when it was all about helping those two become who God created them to be.

I have watched so many sports clips of runners about to cross a finish line in first place who are distracted as they hear the crowd cheering and who start celebrating and then fail to win. We are running a race of our own. We need to stay focused on the finish line and not allow the "crowd"—meaning the world and culture around us—to distract us and cause us to stumble or slow down and let the race be lost. I recognize several phases in my own stretch of single parenting where I became focused on what I wanted or needed more than on finishing the race for my children. In those phases, I can see as I look back, my children lacked what they needed from me to continue to grow and become what God had in mind when he created them. We need to be vigilant about staying the course regardless of how hard the course may seem. I can't go back and correct the times when it seemed I let my children down. I can only move forward with resolve to finish the race set out for me.

> Therefore, since we are surrounded by such a great cloud of witnesses, let us throw off everything that hinders and the sin that so easily entangles. And let us run with perseverance the race marked out for us. (Hebrews 12:1 NIV)

Regardless of the times I know I let my children down, God still wants to give the victory of the race to them and to me. The real struggle comes when we can't take the victory because there is no room in our hands. We allow our hands to be filled with all the things our current culture is telling us we should want. Our hands are already full, so we can't grab hold of the victory God wants to give us! God wants to give us so much more than we are hanging on to. God doesn't force us to put down what we are holding, though. This is where our focus, where we keep our eyes, minds, and hearts, becomes crucial. If we seek to please God and do what is pleasing to him, we can put down all the things we are hanging on to and genuinely enjoy the amazing gifts he is giving us. We need to throw off whatever is hindering us or slowing us down.

I used to worry about what people thought of me and my children when we were out together. Did they wonder where their dad was? It took me awhile to realize people weren't thinking about us. They may have noticed us, but usually the thoughts were about our laughter while we were together. This became clear to me one day in the grocery store. It was the Christmas season, and we found a decoration of three penguins that danced and sang "White Christmas." At the end of the song, the smallest penguin with a bell attached at its neck would begin shaking the bell constantly. We laughed and laughed at that decoration. We got so wrapped up in the laughter that I had to buy the decoration so we could take the laughter home with us. As we played it and laughed over and over, I realized most everyone near us in the store was watching us—and laughing with us. They were completely caught up in our joy and laughing with us. Somehow, God used those silly penguins to help me see that my little family, despite our hurts, could show the abundant joy of living as children of God to the world around us. Abundant joy is what I want people to see when they look at us. I put down my concerns of what people thought that day to pick up sharing the joy of the Lord in all we do as a family.

We will have to put things down and know deep in our hearts that God is giving us everything we need. Focus your attention on what God is doing today and what God will do in the future. We need to put down the distractions that only stop us from having room to take hold of what God offers! This is how we keep our focus on God and avoid focusing on ourselves and what we think we need. I have done a small amount of rock climbing, and a couple of lessons from rock climbing illustrate this perfectly. Regardless of where you are in the climb or how good a handhold on a specific rock might feel, you have to let go of one handhold to reach for another. If you were to refuse to let go of the rock where you are, you couldn't climb any higher. Additionally, you have equipment to support you. A harness and rope system is used to ensure that if you miss the next place you are reaching for, the ropes will catch you. The higher rocks are the good God has for you, and the rope system and harness is God, ready to reach out and pull you back up if you fall.

There will be plenty of days when you feel like you have hit the end of your ability to continue running the race set before you. You don't want to walk on the water; you want to simply climb back into the boat and take a nice long nap. There are days when it seems impossible to carry the load any longer, much less walk across the water toward Jesus. I have had many of those days, days when I felt so completely overwhelmed and overloaded that my only response was to cry out *at*

God, not exactly to God. One day when dealing with a flat tire, a work deadline, children needing to be driven to practices, and dinner that had to be made, I screamed and cried at God, saying, "I hope you are happy! I am completely alone and can't do this anymore!" Somehow despite the flat tire that set off my screaming and crying, I made it through that day, the kids got dinner, and practices were attended. I not only made it through that day but also made it through the many years that came after it. Don't give up hope; keep your eyes fixed on Jesus.

We try to hide our entire struggle. We try to act like everything is absolutely fine and nothing is wrong. We don't want to admit our limitations and our weaknesses. Real faith demands truth with ourselves so we can embrace grace and forgiveness. Real faith demands truth and honesty with others so we can gain help. With honesty I can pray and cry out to God, "I am weak, I am lost, I am lonely, I am angry, I am scared! Help me, Lord, because I doubt myself. I don't know how to be a parent." This is the moment when God can come to me and help me. Fake strength and posturing will only prevent grace from embracing me and hinder my ability to accept the healing and sustaining provisions God wants to give me.

In 1 Kings 19 we read of the prophet Elijah and his conflict with Jezebel. She is seeking his death, and Elijah is on the run.

> He replied, "I have been very zealous for the Lord God Almighty. The Israelites have rejected your covenant, torn down your altars, and put your prophets to death with the sword. I am the only one left, and now they are trying to kill me too." (1 Kings 19:14 NIV)

You can serve God and still feel like you are completely at the end of your rope. You can keep your focus on Jesus and still end up exhausted, especially if you are trying to keep up pretenses of perfection. Following God's purpose and leading doesn't exempt you from being drained and feeling exhausted. You do need to take care of yourself, nurture your spiritual strength, and gain the perspective to know when you need to ask for help and accept help from those God puts into your life. Make sure you take time for daily devotionals and prayer time alone. Make time to be still and listen for God's leading and comfort. Set times for this in your daily schedule like an appointment on your calendar. When our list of things to do becomes more of our focus than our connection with God, we are going to lose our grounding and orientation—and then emotional, physical, and spiritual exhaustion is inevitable. Get in a place where you can be still and hear the still small voice.

The reality is that single parenting is hard. It is very hard. Sure, the joy-filled, fun, and rewarding days far outnumber the hard days. The hard days knock you down flat, and as you try to get up, they hit you again. When we are focused on God and allow him to speak to our hearts, we will know we can call out to him for help. We will know when we need to put down any pride we carry in our hands and accept help from those God has placed around us. Those God blesses us with can become the hands and feet of Christ for us in the most fear-filled times. When my daughter was training for her black belt in American karate, she was inspired by the song "The Climb." I found myself inspired too. For those of us raising kids as single parents, it is the climb. We must fight off the overwhelming pain of loneliness, fear, isolation, hopelessness, and defeat by focusing on the moment. This step in the climb has beauty that will become a treasure in our memories. Even the hardest step to take has beauty. After that incredibly hard step, focus only on the next step. Fix your eyes on Jesus, not the evidence of the wind.

Last summer I had a wonderful day of hiking at Tallulah Falls. While I was hiking I was carefully watching the path and each of my steps so I would not stumble or fall. Then something prompted me to look up. The towering trees and bright blue sky were wonderfully breathtaking! I realized I had only seen half the hike! I had been so careful to watch where each step was placed that I missed the amazing scenery all around me. We need to be aware of the path and our footing, but we must never look down solely. We need to keep the dual focus of where we are and the beautiful view all around us! We need to keep our eyes up and on God so we don't miss the beauty and joy surrounding us.

When we keep our eyes lifted to God and take in the beauty and joy around us, we accomplish multiple things. We gain joy and perspective in our daily living. We also gain the ability to stay above the water line and move toward Jesus. We model for our children that we are children of God filled with hope and joy no matter what the circumstance of the day may be. With our eyes lifted and focused on God, we gain the ability to embrace the blessings God gives us through those we are surrounded by in our communities and our churches. What a blessing to have a tremendous number of Christian friends and church family members who consistently step up to help us. What a joy to demonstrate to my children that the church family is the village that will help me raise them. I know I will continue to need the help of that village for certain.

We will begin to sink at times because we are human, and we will turn our eyes toward the evidence of the storm. We will focus on something other than Jesus. When we start to go under, we can do exactly like Peter and cry out to Jesus, "Lord, save me! I am going under!" He will reach out and pull us up from below the water. Time after time as we make this climb out of the boat and on to the water—as we focus on Jesus and then are distracted by incoming storms and sink—we can call out to him and feel him lift us again and again. I wish I could say in these sixteen years I have gained the ability not to look at the storms and sink. Truth is, I find myself below water just as much now as at any time along this journey. I think feeling strong makes it harder to focus on Jesus. When I am weak I don't sink near as much. We all need to consistently recognize we are weak, and we need to keep our eyes fixed on Jesus. When the storm distracts us, we need to quickly cry out to be pulled back up. Maintaining a perfect focus on Jesus was difficult for Peter, so it is understandably difficult for us.

I have also found I benefit from a developing skill: feet and moisture awareness. The ability of knowing when more than just the bottoms of my feet are getting wet has grown with time and practice. Early in my journey as a solo parent, I wouldn't want to admit I was feeling a little down. I would deny it, push myself, and avoid the hard conversation. I would wait until I was up to my neck in the water and sinking fast before I would cry out. With acceptance of my need for Jesus to be my focus and my source of security, I have learned to notice when my ankles are getting wet and call out then.

The other night I was checking out at the grocery store. I had a dozen roses in my cart with the milk and other groceries. The clerk asked who they were for and then looked a bit surprised when I answered,

"Me." I have learned to see the small subtle signs cropping up telling me the tops of my feet are getting wet, telling me that the loneliness is starting to outweigh the joy. So I take action. My granddad used to tell me roses are God's signature on creation and his way of reminding us the beauty of this world is his gift to us. When I start to feel alone, I buy myself grocery store roses to remind myself of God's love and to bring me joy. It keeps my focus on him. I encourage you to find what works for you to keep your focus on God and not the wind.

When we look at the Israelites, it seems peculiar to us when they grumble at Moses. Moses leads them out of slavery in Egypt and takes them through the Red Sea on dry ground. No sooner has freedom been placed miraculously in front of them than they become impatient waiting for Moses to come back down from the mountain.

The Israelites grumbled at Moses when they encountered hardships and struggles. Often the Israelites wanted to return to slavery instead of living in freedom to avoid the hardships. This is the human condition! We are slaves to grief and anger, sorrow and bitterness, pain and fear. Too many of us would rather remain slaves than face the hardships of escaping those emotions. Many of us don't want to go through the desert of emotional growth and healing that leads us to the promised land of emotional wholeness. When God begins the process of freeing us, we have to pay a price. Despite the sorrow, we have become comfortable in our state of grief. Despite the anger, we find a certain comfort when we are a slave to bitterness. We don't know what will fill the empty space if we let go of our pain. We are truly afraid of the unknown place in front of us. We wonder, *Who will I be as a whole and healthy person?* As ridiculous as it seems, the Israelites rebelled against Moses for removing them from the life of slavery they were accustomed to. Amazingly, many of us are like the Israelites. We have become comfortable with our identity as hurt and damaged people. If we allow God to heal us, we have to give up our damage and to let go of our sorrow and any hurt and anger we are carrying. Sometimes we even fear that if we gain wholeness, we will disrespect the loved one we have lost or make it seem as though the struggle we have been through in our divorce or loss wasn't traumatic. Recovery and healthy living is not disrespectful. Wholeness does not demonstrate that the loss wasn't traumatic. Healthy living and wholeness demonstrates that our God is stronger and bigger than the trauma! We need to put down the hurt and anger and free our hands to take hold of what God is offering us. We are offered an invitation to step out of the boat and participate in miracles every day as we parent our children with God as the head of the household.

Sometimes the evidence of wind taking our eyes off Jesus seems beyond our control. I am speaking of those genuinely difficult situations that generate very real fear. I have spoken to parents who are consistently threatened by the ex-spouse regarding custody matters or financial matters. Or the circumstances where the ex-spouse has a lifestyle or way of living counter to a structured, balanced, and consistent way of living the other parent is trying to provide for the children. When I was speaking about this to one mother, the anguish I saw in her eyes as she spoke of fearing her children would be taken from her was something I will never forget. When I asked her how she managed during those times, her answer was, "Faith." You will not always have a voice in your children's lives that is echoed by others in their lives. If there is another parent, or even a parent–stepparent combination, you may not always have the chance to establish a consistent, pure, and healthy set of discipline expectations. You do have faith and the ability to stand on the convictions you are led by God to maintain. These are real storms, but God is able to keep you on top of the water during these storms.

> Though the fig tree does not bud and there are no grapes on the vines, though the olive crop fails and the fields produce no food, though there are no sheep in the pen and no cattle in the stalls, yet I will rejoice in the Lord, I will be joyful in God my Savior. (Habakkuk 3:17–18 NIV)

Habakkuk gives us a glimpse into how to manage this type of significant struggle. Habakkuk witnessed loss, failure, and disappointment. He struggled through the collapse of nearly all that mattered to him. This afforded him the perspective of what is important and what is transitory. He learned what is actually treasure and what is worthless. His response was that if the fig tree and vine bear no fruit, and if the herds stop producing, he would still praise the Lord. Praising God does not depend on your social status, your success in your endeavors, or the acceptance of your expectations, discipline, plans, and approach by others in your children's' lives. Continually pray for God to help you see what is praiseworthy and good in your life so you can be empowered to praise him regardless of worldly acclaim, approval, or even consistency. If you only have half the voice in your child's life, make certain it is a voice of praise and thanksgiving.

When God speaks and you obey, moving closer to what you are to accomplish for the kingdom, you will experience opposition. Spiritual assaults and attacks by the ungodly are indications you are closer to the center of God's will for your life. Know you are not alone. God loves you. Should you start to sink below the waterline, you only have to reach for his hand, which will be reaching out to catch you!

In the United Methodist Church, a covenant prayer written by John Wesley is used to articulate what it is to surrender all to God. We must strive to live a covenant prayer life.

> I am no longer my own, but thine.
> Put me to what thou wilt, rank me with whom thou wilt.
> Put me to doing, put me to suffering.
> Let me be employed for thee or laid aside for thee, exalted for thee or brought low for thee.
> Let me be full, let me be empty.
> Let me have all things, let me have nothing.
> I freely and heartily yield all things to thy pleasure and disposal.
> And now, O glorious and blessed God, Father, Son and Holy Spirit, thou art mine, and I am thine.
> So be it.
> And the covenant which I have made on earth, let it be ratified in heaven.
> Amen.

If you really examine the content of the prayer, you see that it is a level of submission most of us do not attain in this life. We need to realize this is a part of walking on water. Jesus says to us, "Get out of the boat." We need to respond with complete willingness to climb out of the boat.

> Cast your cares on the Lord and he will sustain you; he
> will never let the righteous be shaken. (Psalm 55:22 NIV)

Surrendering everything means putting down anything you are holding on to that prevents you from taking hold of what God has for you. It means getting out of the boat and getting your feet wet. It also means dying to yourself and doing what is best for your children before you do what is best for you as an individual when God leads you in that direction. It means that if God calls you to stay single, you are willing to stay single, and if God calls you to remarry, you do that and go where he calls you and do what he places before you. As the prayer states, "I surrender all things to thy pleasure and disposal, God!" I am not claiming to have the answer as to whether you should date or not date, remarry or not remarry. That decision is between you and God, and it is a decision that needs to be made with prayer and reflection, not emotion and perceived needs. I have witnessed some amazing examples of surrender in the lives of single parents I have encountered. I once knew a set of parents who were divorced but, for the sake of the children, lived only a few houses apart. They made certain the children would have access to either parent at any time. Both parents made sacrifices to be certain the children had consistency and security as they grew up. Another situation I witnessed was a parent who, after a divorce, chose to stay in the small and less than ideal house the children knew as home to provide consistency for those children. The parent's desire to live in another house was very real, but the desire to make sure the children felt safe and secure was greater. This is what these parents felt led by God to do. This is what surrender looks like. As they continue walking on the water, keeping their eyes on Jesus, the result is an emotionally healthy family.

In thirty years of teaching I have seen students whose lives were destroyed by self-serving parents who put their own romances ahead of their children. These kids are subjected to parents who use financial resources for their own wardrobes and nights out and don't provide some of things the children might need to flourish and develop their talents. These kids tell me they can't have math tutors or music lessons because their parent doesn't have the money, while the parent has the resources for the latest fashions and nights out every week. There are also children who have no one to talk to or to help them establish strong study skills at home because the parent is regularly out on dates. I have also seen examples of amazing children raised in blended families—children who are kind and compassionate to their peers, who have strong work ethics and excellent academic accomplishments as well as stepparents and stepsiblings. The healthy situations consistently have a focus on the One who is calling them to walk on water.

I have spent the past sixteen years allowing God to lead me in this. I have said to others I would know that someone was brought into my life by God if he loved me and my children and would clearly make my life and the lives of my children better. I had the joy of sharing a lunch conversation with a mom who is a faith-guided person and who experienced this. She told me that after her divorce, she was working and raising her two very small children when God placed her husband in her life. She told me the story of when she realized this was of God. Her son, then an infant, needed surgery. She said she had just met and started dating this man and did not expect him to sit with her at the hospital. He did, and then he did more. As her baby was crying and inconsolable, he asked if he could hold him and try to comfort him. As he held her infant son, the crying stopped. Tears came to her eyes as she told me she realized in that moment this man could love her children like they were his own, and she knew. She also said that bringing a person into her life and the lives of her children was scary, but she prayed and felt convicted this was a gift from God. That was about seventeen years ago. She has a happy marriage, and her children are amazing children who love God and are faith-guided teens.

The key component seems to be that those who act in faith, responding to God's leading, are the ones who have raised faith-guided children who are amazing and glorify God in all they do. I have seen divorced parents choose to live in the same neighborhood for the sake of the children. I have seen widowed women wait to date and remarry until their children are all grown. I have seen single moms who date and manage to keep the needs of their children as the first priority. I have seen divorced dads who lead selfless lives to give their children stability and support. I have also witnessed single moms who don't date and are negative and miserable and teach their children to think and act the same way. There are so many complications in the life of a single parent: fear of your children being taken away from you by an ex-spouse, fear you can't provide, fear you will give them too much responsibility, fear you will not give them enough responsibility. The wind blows constantly out here!

The one answer that will not fail you: keep your eyes on Jesus, not the wind.

The apostle Paul stayed in Ephesus against practical wisdom. Ephesus had become hostile toward him, but he knew God had opened doors of service and ministry. Paul felt convicted God was calling him to be there, so he stayed. Paul based his decisions on God's activity rather than on what people were saying and doing. When you are dealing with the many complications that surround you, look beyond what people are saying and seek what God is doing! Look past your emotions and fears, focus on what God is doing in your life and in the lives of your children, and then act by faith.

We are absolutely like Peter, and Jesus has called us out of the boat. We are walking on water! Successful single parenting is genuinely nothing short of a modern miracle. We must keep our eyes focused on Jesus to stay above the waterline. Peter was notorious for saying impetuous things or acting on impulse. One thing we know for certain about Peter: he was seeking to know Jesus and be with Jesus. I think that is why he was so willing to just climb on out of that boat and head across the water. He wanted to be with Jesus enough that he would climb on out. I know God is calling us to shape his children into disciples who long to be with him. That requires of us a willingness to be the ones ready to climb out of the boat and show those children that being out of the boat is the right place for a disciple and that God will sustain them. If my kids can say they saw in me the willingness to get my feet wet for the sake of following Jesus, then I will feel I have modeled the life for them I pray they will have.

The Battle to Choose

For you equipped me with strength for the battle; you made those who rise against me sink under me.
—2 Samuel 22 (ESV)

When I was growing up, the pastor at my childhood church, Rev. Don Smith, would often say this: "When I was young I had three theories on raising children. Now I have three children and no theories!" In many ways, that sums up parenting. When we first become parents, we don't imagine ever being single parents. Yet, here we are doing the very best we can.

When I first became a mom, my mother gave me two motherly pearls of wisdom. The first one was to realize that I would want everyone who met my child to love my child, but that those who met my child would not have to love my child. I would need to raise my child to be lovable through discipline and boundaries. The second pearl of wisdom is really part two of the first one, and it is simple: choose your battles carefully.

I am sitting in a hotel room alone. On the floor above me, directly above me, is my son and his teammates. He has just played two games today, and they are doing what high school boys do—eating junk food, playing video games, and being way too loud. We are at a tournament designed to give college coaches a look at potential recruits. The day involved a win and a tie—and a very positive conversation with a college coach. As I am thinking about the positive direction my son seems to be moving in, I get texts from my daughter. She is asking for guidance as she is running budgets and deciding on a new car and apartment furnishings. She is living alone, working in a growing company in a flourishing field, and happy. She is confident in herself and her ability to take on adult life. Sure, tough days will come again. Today, though, an overwhelming sense of joy washes over me. Almost as intense and thick as the grief I felt when their dad died, this thick wave of joy is generated from an understanding that God has those two! They are his! We are experiencing so many reasons to be thankful.

God is your child's parent—you are co-parenting with God. Keep this clear in your mind. There will be so many times when you have questions, when you want predictions of outcomes. Ultimately, you need to pray for clarity and let God lead your decisions. Let God be the authoritative parent for your children. Establish the boundaries you know God is leading you to establish. Place your priorities where God is showing you to place them. Most of the time this is a step-by-step, follow God one day at a time relationship that does not afford us a clear look at the future. We need to try to live like the disciples did: follow instead of asking questions. You know those disciples had to have a great many questions, but they spent more time in action as they followed Jesus than in conversation. We should strive to live like that. By the power of the Holy Spirit, led by the peace that passes understanding, we can know what God's best is for us and for our children. We can follow without asking for guaranteed outcomes. The exciting truth I can tell you is that sixteen years and more down the road, just following, I can look back and see God's very best was so much better than any decision I would have made if I had been following my own intellect or my own choices. Being led by the Holy Spirit daily is the best way to know where we should be going today. It is the best way to make the decisions your children's heavenly Father would want made for them.

In striving to follow where God will lead, you will need to consistently work to make your relationship with God your most important priority. Place your relationship with God at the top of your priority list, and let your children see you doing this. Model for your children the habits of daily devotional and Bible study. Give your children times to pray with you, and let them know you are in prayer for them. Model for your children how to enjoy earthly relationships while making certain they do not take top priority over your relationship with God. Model wanting God and God's will the very most! This will allow your children to see how they can have a God-centered life and will allow you to co-parent with God.

Your activities need to include study time, prayer time, and quiet time to hear what God is sharing with you as his call. Your purpose is to point your children and those around you to God and God's grace. You have a purpose for the good of the kingdom of God, and so do your children. If you are in union with God, then your priorities become the priorities God has placed on your heart. You are no longer praying for what you want; you are praying for God's will to be done and for your heart to come into alignment with his purpose for you. Your prayer request is to hear his call and move in the direction he leads. This is a game changer. Instead of seeking the path to acclaim and earthly accomplishments, we are seeking what God values and wants for us and for our children. This is a challenge to keep in perspective. If you value success by the world's standards more than your relationship with God, you may be willing to trade your relationship with God for gain. It is hard for us to realize that victory, accomplishments, wealth, and acclaim are not indications of God's presence in our lives. God's presence is more valuable than any of the world's gain. Keep that distinction clear.

No matter how lonely you may feel, you will never be alone, because God is always with you. You will never experience distress greater than God's love for you. No persecution could be so painful that God cannot comfort you. No amount of poverty could strip you of God's protection and provision. You can't base your view of God's love on your circumstances. The death of Christ on the cross validates our belief. We were not promised a pain-free road. We do have a promise of comfort and provision in every circumstance. Instead of evaluating God's love based on your circumstances, evaluate your circumstances through the lens of God's love. This is what it is to coparent your children with God.

I was having lunch with a close friend when she said something profound. She lost her husband to cancer a few years ago. She told me she felt anger and resentment when people told her their spouse was a cancer survivor. She said it hurt when she saw others who won the battle against cancer when her husband had not. I realized then I had a similar challenge. I feel resentment and emotional pain every time I am told by someone about the new love they have found or how they had come through a divorce or been widowed and had found love again. Those stories cause hurt and resentment for me. They heighten my awareness of the pain I feel from the loneliness I carry with me. The platitudes of "someday" and "your turn" are insulting in the light of the pain and loneliness I feel at times. Most days I don't feel aware of loneliness at all. However, I do have days when a moment or a situation will come up that pushes the heartache to the front.

I have to guard my heart from the hard moments that are predictable. When I know a difficult or hurtful situation is coming, I intentionally surround myself with the Christ-centered friends God has placed in my life. I need to do this intentionally so I can continue to make thankfulness and my relationship with God my first priority. God has not promised to make my road easy and loneliness-free. God has promised to be with me every step of the way. Moreover, God has promised to work all things for the good for those who love him. I can't change the circumstances I live in, but I can choose to live well within those circumstances. Sure, I would embrace a change in my circumstances, but I will not sacrifice being in God's will for my life, or risk not placing my children's futures in God's hands. Honestly, sometimes I wish I could google "What is God going to accomplish in my life?" and have the answer show up on the screen instantly—but that is not a life of faith.

Too often we pray and expect a google-speed result. Most of the time the result is not google speed. When that is the case, we will most likely look back and thank God for the delay in his answer. Sometimes we get to walk a road that looked impossible at the start, one step at a time, for eighteen years and then realize God was providing the answer we needed most every step of the way! Our battle is to keep our relationship with God as our first priority so we can continue to follow tomorrow. When we keep our relationship with God at the top of our priority list, we can live out our inner convictions and teach our children to do the same. We can also live confidently knowing that God is going to do what is best for our children and that we do not need to live in fear. It may seem endless right now, but your time in this season with your children is limited and will pass quickly. Keep your focus on God and the grace offered through Jesus Christ. Jesus tells us he has been where we are and knows how to show us where to go from here. Listen to your inner voice, your heart, your intuition. That is the prompting of the Holy Spirit.

There are so many sources of joy, contentment, and fulfillment in our lives, but nothing should be able to bring us the joy, contentment, and fulfillment like our relationship with God does. Circumstances can change, monetary status is fluid, friendships can come and go, but God is constant—and nothing can take your faith away! This is what gives you the foundation for how you parent your children and whom you teach them to turn to as the authority in their lives. As we seek God, our children will learn to do the same. We will be able to lead them to pray for clarity and understanding of God's will instead of their own desires. They will learn to allow God to plant desires to answer his call in their hearts. Joy will be increased beyond anything you have ever imagined. What we know for certain is that God is calling us to invest in our children so they can become who God had in mind when he created them.

So I listen to the teenage boys' ruckus in the hotel room above me and pray prayers of thanksgiving and praise. I raised my children to place them in his will and presence—and they are his. I built into the kitchen wall a tile that has Jeremiah 29:11—"'For I know the plans I have for you,' declares the Lord." The joy I feel ion seeing the scripture built into our kitchen wall and living, growing, and continuing to be fulfilled is immeasurable. The joy and happiness washing over me is indescribable—because I am my children's mom, and God has raised them up more amazingly than I could ever dream. It has been a battle. I have battled loneliness, fear, strong-willed kids, changing culture and social pressures, fatigue, excessive pride, and a gaping hole in my heart left when their dad passed away. I have also battled time constraints as I attempted to raise my children and maintain a professional career. I have battled the simple needs of life as they crowded out the important moments of spiritual nurture and growth.

At one point, I saw this statement on a social media site: "If you could see the size of the blessing coming, you would be able to realize the magnitude of the battle you are fighting." When I read that statement the first time, I was in the midst of battle and didn't completely understand it on a heart level. Now, as the frenzy of battle is slowing and I can see the grown people of faith my children are becoming, I can bring this to a heartfelt level. The blessing I feel in genuinely experiencing the victory of battle is a blessing so grand that I can understand the magnitude of the battle that had to be fought.

This is the battle worth fighting—the battle to lead your children through their childhood and into an adult life that makes faith the cornerstone of their thinking. The battle to fight is to ensure you guide your children to be faithful over being successful. This is absolutely the battle worth fighting and absolutely the only thing deserving of every ounce of energy you have! God is not finished with our children when they head off to college or move out of our house. God still has his hand on them and is moving them forward for the whole of their lives. God is not finished with us either. This time with your children in your home is a season. A new season will come sooner than you think. You will wonder where the years went and wish for one more night of reading a story before your children go to bed. They will call or text and thank you for the skills and perspectives you taught them. They will honor you in the accomplishments they share. I have a precious picture of my daughter in her graduation cap and gown from college holding a sign that says "Thanks, Mom." I have tried to do all I could to fight the important battles for my children, and I am thankful God is still moving them forward. The exciting news is that God is also moving us forward and that the new season coming will be fantastic for us as well.

My mom used to say, "Choose your battles carefully." She is wise, and I am glad I listened. In one of the first few varsity high school football games my son played, the opponent was a high school football program that is legendary. Our little high school had played them every year since our school opened more than twenty years before, and we never won. Now my son, at age fifteen, was out there facing this team. He successfully kicked his first varsity field goal in that game and scored the first three points of the game. His school team was ahead 3–0, and it was his kick that put those points up there. I took a picture of the scoreboard! Our underdog team went on to win and beat the legendary team for the first time ever. The elation in the stands defied description. As the players, the cheerleaders, the drill team, and a few students who had already run out on the field sang the school alma mater, I cried tears of joy and took more pictures. Then the song ended and the students rushed out on the field to congratulate their team. A huge mob of students celebrating covered the field. The players were celebrating, and the elation in the stands spilled out on to the field as more students and parents joined the celebration. Then I saw something I hope I never forget. My son pushed through the crowd and was walking toward the stands and away from the celebration. He was looking up into the sea of cheering parents. He was looking for me to share this unbelievable moment with. He wanted to make sure he found me. That was the moment he spoke for himself and his sister, saying loud and clear: *I know you have fought the battle, Mom, and you won! You picked the right battle to fight—to go into battle for me and for my sister—and you won! Thank you, Mom, for all you gave up for me and for my sister!*

I know he wasn't actually thinking all that. Nevertheless, his action in that moment said it just the same because my high-school-age son wanted to make sure his victory was mine as well. He wanted to make sure the celebration included his biggest fan and most ardent supporter.

I have given my all to fight the good fight, I have pushed myself to run the good race, and I definitely chose the right battle. I am so thankful. Every sacrifice I made, everything I did not do for myself, every time I did not get to do what I wanted to but instead did what my children needed me to do, all of those fade completely out of sight when for a moment the crowd in the stands went out of focus and I felt so much joy as I saw my son looking for me in the stands. Choose your battles carefully; spend your energy on going into battle for your children. Someday, in a way you least expect, they will thank you.

About the Author

———◇———

Julie Ann Allen is an Ordained United Methodist minister, and is in her 31st year as a public school teacher. She has a Bachelor of Music Education from Baylor University, a Master of Music in Choral Conducting from San Diego State University, and Graduate Theological Studies (CTS) from Brite Divinity School at Texas Christian University. In 2002 Julie Ann was widowed, leaving her with a young child and an infant. She raised her two children while teaching and working in ministry. She has published "You Only Think God Is Silent" and serves as an inspirational speaker. She currently lives in the Dallas Fort Worth area where she is most often seen cheering in the stands at the high school sporting events, or in the high school auditorium applauding for the choir.

Printed in the United States
By Bookmasters